# Using Mindfulness Skills in Everyday Life

In the last decade, more mental health treatments have begun to incorporate mindfulness as a skill to help people with their problems. Despite this, not everyone is sure how to incorporate mindfulness effectively into their daily lives. Giving simple explanations, examples and exercises, *Using Mindfulness Skills in Everyday Life* shows clearly how this is done.

This book, written by two NHS clinicians experienced in teaching mindfulness, takes a down-to-earth approach, providing straightforward answers to the most commonly asked questions. The authors give definitions of mindfulness and guide people through instructions on how to set up and evaluate simple practices. As each component is taught, they provide examples of real-life situations, so the reader can clearly see how to be more mindful as they face the ups and downs of modern living.

This practical guide is essential reading for anyone who wants to learn mindfulness to help with difficulties and challenges. It is also the perfect book for therapists, coaches, teachers, social workers, nurses, psychiatrists and psychologists to recommend to their clients. The book is ideal for students on clinical training courses.

**Dr Christine Dunkley** is
with 30 years' NHS expe

UK, Europe and America on Dialectical Behaviour Therapy, supervision and mindfulness. An honorary lecturer for Bangor University and Clinical Director at Grayrock, Christine trains clinical teams in the UK and abroad. She co-founded the UK and Ireland Society for Dialectical Behaviour Therapy in 2012.

**Dr Maggie Stanton** is a Consultant Clinical Psychologist. She has previously led a Psychological Therapies Department in the NHS, and now focuses on training, supervision and consultancy in the UK, Europe, USA and Australia. She presents on mindfulness and other topics. Maggie is a visiting lecturer at the University of Southampton, a Clinical Lead in a major research trial and Director of Stanton Psychological Services.

# Using Mindfulness Skills in Everyday Life
## A Practical Guide

*Christine Dunkley and
Maggie Stanton*

Routledge
Taylor & Francis Group

LONDON AND NEW YORK

First published 2017
by Routledge
2 Park Square, Milton Park, Abingdon, Oxon OX14 4RN

and by Routledge
711 Third Avenue, New York, NY 10017

*Routledge is an imprint of the Taylor & Francis Group, an informa business*

*British Library Cataloguing in Publication Data*
A catalogue record for this book is available from the British Library

*Library of Congress Cataloging-in-Publication Data*
Names: Dunkley, Christine, author. | Stanton, Maggie, author.
Title: Using mindfulness skills in everyday life : a practical guide /
    Christine Dunkley and Maggie Stanton.
Description: New York : Routledge, 2016. | Includes index.
Identifiers: LCCN 2016005963 | ISBN 9781138930834 (hardback) |
    ISBN 9781138930841 (pbk.) | ISBN 9781315676326 (ebook)
Subjects: LCSH: Self-perception. | Mindfulness (Psychology) | Conduct of life.
Classification: LCC BF697.5.S43 D778 2016 | DDC 158.1—dc23
LC record available at https://lccn.loc.gov/2016005963

ISBN: 978-1-138-93083-4 (hbk)
ISBN: 978-1-138-93084-1 (pbk)
ISBN: 978-1-315-67632-6 (ebk)

Typeset in New Century Schoolbook
by Apex CoVantage, LLC

# Dedication

For John, Laura and Lucy
*Christine*

For Neville, Josh and Jemima
*Maggie*

# Contents

# Contents

# About the authors

**Dr Christine Dunkley** began her career in the NHS in 1982 as a medical social worker specialising in trauma. Her interest in self-inflicted injury brought her into contact with many clients with Borderline Personality Disorder. Because of the prevalence of childhood sexual abuse in this client group, she undertook additional training in counselling and subsequently in Dialectical Behaviour Therapy (DBT) – a mindfulness-based cognitive therapy. In addition to teaching clients mindfulness within DBT, she ran mindfulness groups for the patients of two community mental health teams. In 2006, she was recruited to the national training team for DBT.

Christine now works as an international consultant psychotherapist, having produced over 20 publications on mindfulness, supervision and therapy in the UK, Europe and America. She co-founded the Society for DBT in the UK and Ireland, which accredits DBT therapists and has achieved a Shared Learning Award from the National Institute of Health and Care Excellence (NICE) for work on Counselling in Primary care. She is clinical director for the mental health training company Grayrock and an honorary lecturer for Bangor University. She was on the development team for a new therapy for Treatment Resistant Depression, helping to recruit, train and supervise clinicians for a multi-site NHS trial. She has also served on the national expert reference group for personality disorders. Her latest project is training therapists in a 5-year implementation of DBT across the whole of Ireland, sponsored by the Irish government under the suicide prevention initiative.

**Dr Maggie Stanton** started her career in the nursing profession at St Bartholomew's Hospital, London. She became increasingly interested in the psychological consequences of physical problems and studied psychology at degree level before undertaking her Master of Science in Clinical Psychology at the University of Birmingham and Doctorate in Clinical Psychology at the University of Surrey. In 30 years of mental health clinical work, she has specialised in seeing clients with severe and enduring mental health problems.

As a Consultant Clinical Psychologist and Psychological Therapies Lead, for many years, Maggie headed a team of psychologists and psychological therapists in a large NHS Foundation Trust. Her interest in mindfulness began when she undertook core training in DBT. She developed her mindfulness practice including teaching clients in both individual and group settings, as well as providing supervision, training and support to professionals within her trust and in the wider health care system. She is a visiting lecturer at the University of Southampton on the Doctorate in Clinical Psychology and has been involved in a range of research publishing her work in journals, books and at conferences. Most recently, she is a Clinical Lead in a multi-centred randomised control trial (RCT) for Treatment Resistant Depression. She is a member of the national DBT training team and a Director of the UK and Ireland Society for DBT. She now focuses on providing supervision, training and consultancy internationally and in the UK. As a Director of Stanton Psychological Services, she travels widely, presenting workshops on mindfulness and other topics. She is an accredited practitioner with the British Association for Behavioural and Cognitive Psychotherapies (BABCP), registered with the Health Professions Council, a Chartered Psychologist with the British Psychological Society and a member of the Division of Clinical Psychology.

# Preface

We have written this practical guide for anyone who wants to learn and use mindfulness skills, particularly those who have a problem or difficulty they are trying to overcome. The book came about after the success of our previous book *Teaching Clients to Use Mindfulness Skills: A practical guide* (Dunkley and Stanton) and our workshops of the same name. Experienced mindfulness teachers who liked our teaching style asked for a book they could recommend that would introduce the main principles of learning mindfulness and describe how this skill can be used in everyday situations.

Throughout the book, we have used the term 'mindfulness teacher' on the understanding that it will relate to the many diverse fields in which mindfulness is taught. This book is intended for any person who is learning mindfulness either from an experienced practitioner or from this book.

We have presented the different topics in the order we would introduce them when teaching these skills. Some readers will want to start at the beginning of the book and work their way through, and others will want to dip into certain chapters to discover more about one particular aspect of learning mindfulness. Either way, we hope that the key tasks summarised at the end of each chapter will make this book a valuable resource to keep at hand.

# Acknowledgements

We would like to give our heartfelt thanks to all the clients who helped us hone and develop our skills in teaching mindfulness so that we could share these insights with others. Their courage and determination to use mindfulness in their lives has been a constant source of inspiration.

We would also like to thank both our colleagues at work and delegates who have attended our workshops. Their feedback, humour and support have been immense, and we would not have had the courage to write this book without that. We are grateful to the national and international DBT trainers who have shared their wisdom with us and from whom we have learned such a lot, particularly Marsha Linehan, Heidi Heard, Michaela Swales, Tom Lynch, Jennifer Sayrs and Sue Clarke. We also appreciate Laura's help with the indexing, and would like to thank Vivien, Anne, Louise and Jemima for their generosity of time in commenting on our final draft. Lastly, but very far from least, we would like to give a special thank-you to Neville and John. Without doubt, their advice, encouragement and unstinting faith in us enabled this book to be written.

We use numerous case vignettes throughout this book. These are based on our knowledge and experience over many years, but the examples are fictitious, and no resemblance to any person is intended.

# List of abbreviations

| | |
|---|---|
| BABCP | British Association for Behavioural and Cognitive Psychotherapies |
| CMHT | Community Mental Health Team |
| DBT | Dialectical Behaviour Therapy |
| MBCT | Mindfulness-Based Cognitive Therapy |
| MBSR | Mindfulness-Based Stress Reduction |
| MRI | Magnetic Resonance Imaging |
| NICE | National Institute of Health and Care Excellence |
| RCT | Randomised Control Trial |

# What is mindfulness?

Do you ever worry about things that may happen and end up feeling stressed or anxious? Does this get in the way of you doing something you want to do? Does it sometimes feel that life is rushing past and you are missing spending time with friends or family? Do you endlessly replay in your mind a mistake you have made or a situation you wish had gone differently? If so, then mindfulness has something to offer you.

So what is mindfulness? The essence of any description will tell you that mindfulness is being awake and aware of the present moment, choosing where to put our attention, noticing when we have got caught up in our mind's story of how life is and bringing our attention back to the here and now. Once we have this skill, we can choose when we use it, and it's amazing what a difference this can make; it can be invaluable as in the example below:

### Using mindfulness at work

Amy got an email from her boss saying that he wanted to see her. She began thinking that he would tell her that her job was under threat. She imagined that he was unhappy with the standard or speed of her work. As she walked to his office, with her heart racing and mouth dry, she remembered her mindfulness practice. She recognised that being caught up in why her boss wanted to see her was not being mindful. She brought her focus onto the experience of walking along the corridor, with the carpet under her shoes and the sound of people talking from the offices. When Amy 'woke up' to realise she was paying attention to her minds' version of events, she was being mindful. In noticing her experience of walking along the corridor, she brought her attention into the present moment.

From this example, we can see Amy's mind went to an imagined future (her boss being unhappy with her work). When she realised this and brought her attention back to the moment of walking down the corridor, she was being mindful.

## Automatic pilot

An example of being unmindful or mindlessness that you may find easy to recognise is when we are on 'automatic pilot', that is, doing things without being aware of what we are doing.

I work in two locations during the week: the clinic and the university. The first part of the journey is the same. Sometimes I can set off for the university, and before I realise it, I am turning into the clinic. I have been driving on automatic pilot. If I had been driving mindfully, I would have been aware of where I was, the road in front of me, changing gear, and would have gone to my intended destination.

Has this, or something like it, ever happened to you? Of course, this process is a very natural thing that all minds do. But how much of the time do you live in 'automatic pilot' rather than fully living each moment? Might it make a difference to your life to learn to be mindful?

## Taking control of your mind

We first came to mindfulness through our work as therapists when we trained to deliver Dialectical Behaviour Therapy (DBT). Marsha Linehan developed this therapy, and she makes the point that mindfulness puts you in the driver's seat so that you are in control of your mind, rather than your mind being in control of you. So what does your mind being in control of you mean? Here are a couple of examples.

> Rob had been struggling at college. He'd failed a couple of assignments and was finding it hard to sit down and write his essay. Whenever he sat at the computer, his mind would go back over all the assignments he'd failed in the past or onto predicting that this one would fail too. It was so powerful that Rob couldn't even start the essay he needed to do. The chatter of Rob's mind was taking him away from the course he wanted to follow. He didn't ask it to do this. He wanted to get the work done and to do well.

> Cheryl hadn't heard from her friend and thought 'I must have done something to upset her.' Whenever she had the urge to text or phone her friend, she would put it off. The longer it went on, the more convinced she was by thoughts that her friend was angry with her and didn't want to see her.

We can't stop our minds from producing thoughts like this. Minds churn out thoughts like sweat glands produce sweat, but if we have the skill of being mindful, we can notice what our mind is doing and bring it back to what we *want* to focus on, so that we can write the essay or text our friend. We are in the driver's seat and it feels good!

## The growth of mindfulness

In 1979, Jon Kabat-Zinn started using mindfulness with his patients in a stress reduction programme. He noticed people often live their lives thinking about what *might* happen in the future or what *has* happened in the past and treating these thoughts as if they are facts. He was aware that eastern meditative practices such as Buddhism focus on bringing attention into the present moment, accepting it rather than trying to push it away or make it into something different. He thought this could be a helpful skill for the patients he was working with, so he introduced it into his programme. Jon Kabat-Zinn is credited with being the first person to bring mindfulness into Western clinical practices. In the following years, mindfulness has been incorporated into many therapies for a variety of problems. A common theme in these therapies is the emphasis on changing our relationship to experiences rather than changing the experiences themselves. It would be great if we could go through life having only positive things happen wouldn't it? But we know that's not realistic. Of course if we can change something, let's go ahead, but how many things happen that we cannot change, at least not immediately? Accepting the experience without judging it as good or bad allows us to have the experience and choose how we want to respond to it. The changes for people can be truly remarkable, enabling them to start doing activities they had previously given up or going into situations they had been avoiding. In Chapter 8 we tell the stories of how people have used mindfulness in this way.

Research into mindfulness has grown at a tremendous pace. Its application has expanded from medicine and psychology to education, sport, business and leadership. The merging of the two great traditions of empirical science and Buddhist meditative practice has provided a catalyst for the expansion of mindfulness into many areas, and there is growing evidence for its beneficial effects.

## Brain changes

One area of research that has generated a lot of interest is looking at whether mindfulness meditation has an impact on the brain. Many people will have seen pictures taken with Magnetic Resonance Imaging (MRI) scanning of brain activity changing when a person engages in mindful meditation. An example was shown on BBC News (4.1.12, BBC News). A patient with chronic pain was taught mindfulness meditation. When meditating, the scans showed a decrease in her brain activity in areas associated with pain. This fitted with her experience of the pain being more manageable or 'being taken down a notch' when using mindfulness meditation.

Does this mean mindfulness is for everyone? Research has also looked at whether people suffer any negative effects. If we think of mindfulness as a skill of directing where we put our attention and bringing ourselves into the actual moment of our lives, then it is hard to see that this is going to prove hugely detrimental. There are suggestions that practices should be kept short initially, that if you are learning from a teacher, they should be properly qualified, supervised and have their own practice, and if you have physical or mental health problems, to seek advice, for example, from a medical practitioner. So whilst no one skill is for everyone, a balanced view is needed remembering mindfulness is being taught in schools and used widely in therapies, business and sport with growing evidence of positive gains.

## Our experience

Our approach to teaching mindfulness is that it is a *practical skill* that can be learned and used in many different situations. This may be slightly different to other books that you have seen on this topic. We are experienced NHS therapists who have helped many people use mindfulness skills to overcome their difficulties, some of which were very severe. People we worked with were often desperate, unable to see how anything could change. We had the privilege of being able to teach these people mindfulness skills and how to apply them not only during the time they spent with us in formal teaching, but during their daily activities at home and at work. The results were often life-changing, and for some, life-saving. The feedback about the way we taught mindfulness was so good that other therapists were interested in our style of teaching. Over the last 6 years, we have taught thousands of therapists in our workshops, showing how to bring the skill of mindfulness into people's lives in an accessible and useful way.

Reading this book is your opportunity to hear our top tips and suggestions for learning mindfulness. You can be confident that the things we suggest have been tried in the most challenging circumstances. If mindfulness can help in those situations, then it probably has something to offer you too. If you are thinking, 'this doesn't sound like me, I don't have any particular problems or issues,' then don't put the book aside. These strategies and practices are relevant to all of us. We have found mindfulness hugely beneficial to us. Everyone is subjected to the influence of their own mind, and we will teach you how to become awake and aware of how that process works. We continue to do the same practices that we teach to others, and we share in the same benefits of leading a more mindful life. In the following chapters, we will show you how to develop and use this skill to enhance your work, your relationships and your experience of being comfortable in your own skin. If that sounds like it's for you, then read on!

## Developing our own practice

In order to learn the skill of being mindful, it's no surprise that we need to practise it. Any skill needs to be developed if it's going to be useful to us, whether it's riding a bike or boiling an egg. So like us, you will need to incorporate a regular time to be mindful into each day. This can be anything from a couple of minutes to much longer times, but it is helpful to start small and build up. Often people will set aside a short time when they first get up, come home from work or before they go to bed. To learn mindfulness, you need to have a time to practise, and we will talk more about setting up your formal practice time in the next chapter. We like to practise both on our own and with others. You may also want to consider joining a mindfulness group or class where you can take part in mindfulness together and help each other in learning this valuable skill. We have found having our own mindfulness practice not only has had a huge impact on us being able to incorporate mindfulness into our lives, but is also an important part of our ability to teach mindfulness to others.

You may notice we use personal examples in this book. We do this because people have told us they like it, and it helps them to see how they could use mindfulness in their lives. It also demonstrates that we are no different; we need to use the skills as much as anyone does.

## What will mindfulness do for me?

You may have picked up this book because you have heard about mindfulness from a friend or colleague, watched a clip on YouTube or read about it on the internet or in the paper and are curious to find out more. Or it could be that you are having difficulties, and it has been suggested that mindfulness may be useful to you. You may have been given this book by your therapist or mindfulness teacher. Some of you may have practised meditation or yoga and are interested in expanding the benefits you have gained. Whatever the reason, we hope you will enjoy reading this book and trying out the mindfulness practices in it.

Learning mindfulness as a skill means that you can use it when you want to, whether that is to get more out of events you are enjoying or to help when life gets tough. Let's give you an example:

A member of our mindfulness class, Alana, told us about going to the pub with her friends Rachel and Sarah for an evening out. She knew Sarah had also been to mindfulness classes and practised it regularly. Sarah had been shouted at by a customer that day at work and kept going over how unpleasant they had been to her and what she wished she had thought to say to them at the time. Alana and Rachel were sympathetic, but Sarah became more upset each time she remembered the event. Eventually Alana said: 'Sarah, your mind keeps going back to what happened at work today and it's stopping you from enjoying the evening. This could be a good time to use the mindfulness you have learned. Just notice when your mind wanders and bring it back to being in the pub with me and Rachel and what we are talking about now.' 'That's not the mindfulness I have done,' said Sarah. 'When I do mindfulness, I go up to my room for half an hour, and everyone in the house is quiet while I do it, and I feel a lot better afterwards.'

Sarah is obviously willing to practice regularly and is getting benefit from doing this, which is great. But by only doing the mindfulness practices in her room, and not using mindfulness in her everyday life, she is missing out on all the extra benefits she could have. By learning how to use mindfulness in everyday situations, Sarah could have noticed when her mind went back to what happened at work that day, gently brought her attention back to the conversation and enjoyed the evening with her friends.

In this book, our aim is to show you how to be able to use mindfulness in your life when you want to. We will take you through the steps of how to carry out, reflect on and learn from short practices, and then how to use your mindfulness skills in your everyday life. We finish each chapter with some key tasks we suggest you try out as you go along. So start the journey.

## Key tasks

• Read on!

# 2

# Why learn mindfulness skills?

If you have read about mindfulness, seen it on the TV or had this skill suggested to you, you might be wondering what all the fuss is about. If so then keep reading, we hope to explain how this skill might help you in your everyday life.

Ask yourself this question: do you ever try to concentrate on something that you either really want to do or really need to do, only to find that your mind gets pulled away to problems that simply can't be solved in the next 5 minutes, no matter how much you chew them over? It's not even as if all that time you spent worrying or replaying past hurts was fruitful, or allowed you to put these horrible events behind you forever. Most of the time, that kind of 'mind-chug' just gets in the way of you living your life, right?

Do you ever find that things are going reasonably well and then your mind seizes on some issue that you can't seem to let go of, and your mood plummets? Do you ever feel like you are constantly watching yourself, worrying about getting things right, judging yourself harshly?

Here's another question – whenever you have found yourself caught up in worry thoughts, was it your *choice* to spend your time this way? Or did you feel powerless to stop it? Do you feel you have the ability to consciously direct where you want your mind to go, or is it more a case of the tail wagging the dog? Of course, if what you really wanted to do was worry, or judge yourself harshly or ruminate, then you have no need to change anything. But if you feel that sometimes your mind has a mind of its own, then read on; in this chapter, we hope to explain how mindfulness can help you with these problems.

There are so many different ways to learn mindfulness, and reading this book is a good start. It is possible to begin understanding mindfulness through books, tapes and DVDs, many of which are available on the internet. When we ourselves started as students of mindfulness, we were very eager, and sought out classes where we could hone our skills. We learned alongside people who were as keen as us and found that we gained a lot from the more experienced practitioners. We also encouraged each other. So if you can attend a class with a teacher, then we would suggest that you do so.

Whether you are going to attend classes or not, you are going to want to understand what mindfulness could do for you. If you are learning mindfulness as part of a treatment, then it might be because you have a health problem like chronic pain or depression. Perhaps you have come to mindfulness because you have difficulty regulating your emotions. Some people feel emotional pain more deeply than others, or find their emotions flare up quickly, hanging around for longer than usual. It may be that you have been beset by a number of life-stresses that if they had happened one at a time would have been bearable, but all together overwhelm you. It could be that your work and family life create huge demands on you, and you feel you are constantly being pulled in different directions.

If you are already stretched to your limit, mindfulness may seem at best irrelevant and at worst ridiculous. It makes perfect sense that if you are already stressed out, you don't really want to take on any new activities unless you can be sure that there will be a pay-off. Here are some of the reasonable arguments we have heard for holding back from learning mindfulness skills:

1 I've tried loads of new things and none of them have helped: I don't want to expend precious energy on something only to be disappointed.
2 How can sitting in a room listening to a bell or gazing at a candle help with real-world problems? It looks like a big non-event to me.

3  I signed up for another treatment like CBT or DBT, and now I'm being told I need to do this, I can't see why.
4  I have such an enormous amount of distress that when I'm offered something that frankly looks like nothing much, I feel like I'm being fobbed off.

These are actually very valid obstacles, and to try and talk you out of them might in some way invalidate the truth that lies behind them. If we are being truly mindful, we can accept that these obstacles exist and will make it harder to learn the skill. They might even prevent you from doing so. Below is an example from a case where the person did go on to learn mindfulness despite early misgivings:

Jamie had suffered a knee injury that had prematurely ended a promising sporting career. He could not engage in activities without dwelling on how his disability had changed his life. He ruminated constantly on both the physical state of his knee and his past sporting achievements. He would not go out with friends, and talked frequently to his family about his loss. Counselling had helped with the trauma of the injury itself, but he still kept going over and over things in his mind and tried to avoid feelings of sadness or anger. When discussing the possibility of attending sessions to learn mindfulness, Jamie said he could not see how this could help, as his problems were unchangeable – his knee would still be painful and he would not have reached his sporting potential. The mindfulness teacher agreed that this was indeed a set of problems with no obvious solution. Also that she could not see how mindfulness could change either of those things. She said that this seemed to be causing Jamie a lot of emotional pain and wondered where on his body this manifested itself. He pointed to his chest and she asked what he did when he noticed this pain. He told her that he began thinking of the cause of it, diverting his attention back to his knee and to his situation. The mindfulness teacher acknowledged how exhausting this must be. She said that the mindfulness classes were weekly and that she could totally understand the cost to

Jamie of attending; the energy involved in getting there, perhaps increasing his physical pain. She observed that this was
a big ask with no guarantees that mindfulness would deliver
any relief.

At no time does the mindfulness teacher attempt to sway
Jamie in his thinking. She has unhooked from trying to solve
the problem and has even let go of the idea of encouraging
him to come to class. She is modelling a mindful approach
by accepting things as they are. In doing so, Jamie could see
that she was not simply trying to force him to do something
new and that she totally got the measure of his pain. He
became curious because he thought, *well, she is being honest
about what mindfulness is NOT going to do for me, yet she
still seems to think there is something in it, and I want to find
out what that is.* This is exactly the way to approach learning this skill, with an open mind and gentle curiosity, not
being pushed or harangued, and without any false promises.
Jamie's mindfulness coach refrained from giving further
details about any potential benefits until he asked for them.

Jamie did eventually complete a course of eight sessions,
and whilst he continued to experience pain in his knee, his
rumination decreased enough for him to start going out with
his friends. At the end of his sessions, he said, *'looking back
I can't believe how something that seemed so little could give
me so much, but I know I would never have tried it if I had
felt forced into it.'* We cannot know what might have happened if the mindfulness teacher's opening gambit had been
to describe enthusiastically how mindfulness might improve
things, but it is possible that such conviction would have left
Jamie feeling misunderstood.

## Mindfulness is a skill

Some people are cautious about learning mindfulness because
they associate it with Buddhism or eastern meditative
practices.

You may have seen mindfulness leaders with a Tibetan
singing bowl, which is a recognised symbol of eastern

spirituality. In our experience, there are mixed responses to the origins of mindfulness. For a number of people, the fact that mindfulness has been practised for centuries makes it more appealing. They are deeply respectful of the cultural and spiritual background, valuing it over the scientific evidence. On the other hand, some people are quite suspicious about the religious or foreign connections and consider it all 'a bit weird'. One of our participants announced to the group that when he initially started mindfulness, he was very uncertain about 'this voodoo stuff', but that it had turned out to be really helpful.

We teach mindfulness as *a practical skill* that can be learned and used in many different areas of life. We have already highlighted some of the research underpinning the growth in mindfulness-based approaches. If you are interested, you can get copies of articles and a simple Google search will throw up pages of references. There are some informative videos on YouTube and a number of websites explaining both the origins and functions of mindfulness. We have given you some suggestions for recommended reading in the bibliography at the end of this book.

Occasionally, when we have come together with other mindfulness teachers, we have encountered the view that the spiritual origins of mindfulness have been underplayed and that the contribution made by eastern religions has been hijacked by Western academics. Our aim, therefore, is not to overstate or understate either the spiritual or scientific components, but to lay out factual information so that you can make up your own mind. We are deeply respectful both of the origins of this ancient discipline and the scientifically researched benefits it can bring to our health and well-being.

So if mindfulness is a skill then once you have learned how to do it, you can choose whether to use it or not. For example, being able to drive a car does not prevent us from using public transport. A skill is something that has to be learned and practised over time rather than something that can be done immediately. If you worry a lot about getting things right, you will need to know that learning mindfulness is a process of trial and error, where we gradually shape our behaviour so that the skill becomes automatic. Whether you are learning alone or attending classes, you will be committing time and energy to practise in your everyday life. The more you put in, the more you will get out.

In Chapter 1, we gave some definitions of mindfulness, and it is useful to come back to some key phrases to act as reminders. We do not want to get too wordy here, as mindfulness is essentially about experiencing.

- 'Mindfulness means paying attention in a particular way: on purpose, in the present moment. And non-judgementally' (Jon Kabat-Zinn, 1994, p. 4).
- Being mindful is the opposite of being absent-minded or on autopilot.
- Mindfulness is 'Learning to be in control of your own mind instead of letting your mind be in control of you' (Linehan, 1993, p. 65).

## How mindfulness might be helpful

Most people want the answer to the following question, 'How will this help me in my everyday life?' Here is a personal example that you might be able to relate to:

When I am invited to a social event such as a party, I usually say yes, thinking it will be fun. But as the date draws closer, my mind begins to follow a familiar track – it says, 'Do you really want to go? You've been so busy lately, you'll be tired by 10, it will be a chore to get ready and go out, it would be rude to leave early, but what will you talk about? It won't be much fun at all.' I then have an urge to ring up and give my apologies. If I am being unmindful, I will act on those urges. If I am mindful, however, I can identify that all of this is just 'thought traffic', and then I can unhook from it more easily. Needless to say when I ignore this uninvited mind content and go to the party, I usually enjoy myself.

As teachers, we like to give personal examples because we and our students are all in the same boat. Our minds are just doing what minds do. If you are learning with a mindfulness teacher, he or she will practise the exercises along with you, and give examples from their own practice. You will have noticed that from the start, we begin to use language that encourages you to step back from the content of your mind. For example, we have used the phrase 'thought traffic'. We might have described the content of your mind like 'mind-TV', to which one of our students memorably responded, 'yes, and mine shows a lot of repeats.'

Here is an example from someone who was learning mindfulness as part of therapy:

Lauren had a problem with overspending and was heavily in debt. On one occasion, she had just bought a coat that she could not really afford. Back at home, she began to regret her purchase. The coat was still in the bag, unworn, and she had the receipt. The best thing to do, she decided, was to take it back to the shop. But when the time came, her mind started to say, 'What if they don't believe you haven't worn it? What if it is the same girl who served you in the first place? She might challenge you, if anyone in the shop recognises you they will think you are odd or stupid, they may guess that you're in debt; it will be embarrassing and horrid.' She began to feel her chest tighten and her stomach churn. So she did not return the coat. Although this relieved her anxiety in the short term, now her level of debt is keeping her awake at night.

As an introduction to mindfulness, Lauren's therapist said, 'It looks like the actions of your mind prevented you from doing what you really wanted to do. Would it have been helpful if you could have unhooked from those thoughts in order to return your coat to the shop? But I can see how easy it was to get caught up in the content of your mind; those thoughts are very powerful. Mindfulness might help you to do more of the activities you really need to do. Have there been any other times when your mind stopped you doing something?'

Lauren went on to say that she had wanted to apply for a job, but her mind kept saying that she'd never get work because no one would employ her.

Does it ever happen to you as it did for Lauren that your mind prevents you from doing something you set out to do? If so, mindfulness has plenty to offer you.

## Mindfulness metaphors

We hope that by now you're thinking you would like to find out more, so what does mindfulness involve? Here are our favourite analogies to explain what we do when we are being mindful – the first two are well-known metaphors that we've heard on courses, and the second two we devised ourselves:

### The spotlight of your attention:

Imagine that your mind is like a huge spotlight, shining your attention onto a variety of objects throughout the day. We can't turn off the spotlight – it is always on; even when we are asleep it focuses on our dreams. But we can learn how to manoeuvre the spotlight around. We can move the spotlight of our attention to a focus of our own choosing, rather than leave the spotlight to shine randomly. The spotlight is often unwieldy and heavy to turn, and it may swing back when we try to move it. But gradually we can acquire the skill of moving it back to the most effective view. If you are trying to walk a tightrope in the dark, it would be more effective to illuminate the rope than the drop. If we are in a job interview, it is more helpful to focus on answering the questions than remembering previous interviews that went badly.

### The untrained puppy:

Your mind is like an untrained puppy running around wherever it wants, following interesting smells, digging up your flower beds, burrowing under your fence. We can't train a puppy by just holding it still, or putting it in a box. Instead we need to notice where it has gone to, and teach it to come back when we call. It will always wander off at times, but we can bring it under our control. As we start to exercise some control, the puppy will still run off, and we have to be patient and gentle with it, being willing to call it back many times until it learns to respond more quickly to our command.

### The radio receiver:

Until I learned mindfulness, I used to believe that my mind was like a radio receiver where I would be forced to tune in on waking, and then be stuck with whatever was being broadcast for the rest of the day. I had no idea that I could turn up the volume on some things, turn down the volume on others, and even change channels. In mindfulness, we try to turn up the volume on the present moment, and turn down the volume on the past or future. We can even learn to tune out distracting or unhelpful thoughts or feelings.

### The mental muscle:

We cannot stop our mind going off on thoughts that are not of our choosing. But when we notice it has gone and deliberately guide it back, it is like exercising a mental muscle. So if your mind wanders 20 times in the space of 1 minute, and you guide it back 20 times, you have done 20 units of exercise – like 20 press-ups for the mind. So you do not need to worry if your mind wanders many times: every time you guide it back, you increase your mindfulness skill.

The most common response from people to one of these metaphors is to say, 'My mind wanders off all the time.' We're always pleased to hear that because it means we are all completely normal.

Why does our mind wander off so much? It's because the role of the mind is to 'mind' you. That is, to look out for you to see that nothing goes wrong. Let's imagine that you are walking down the street with a friend. You might wander along casually, enjoying the scenery and chatting as you go. But if you were to employ that friend to 'mind' you, like a bodyguard, then your walk might be very different. Crowds, bushes, parked cars might be viewed with suspicion as your minder hurries you past. There would be no opportunity to chat. Your mind sometimes behaves this way, choosing to focus on insignificant things in case they suggest danger. This made sense during evolution, when a rustle in the bushes might indicate an approaching predator, but it is not so helpful now that there are fewer physical threats around. So there is no need to criticise your mind for doing its job. Sometimes, there is a genuine need to protect you – when you're about to cross the road, or a mugger tries to grab your bag. This is the same for all of us. Our ancestors probably survived because our minds had the capacity to look out for us in this way. We just need to notice what our mind is doing and realise that we don't always have to act on its advice.

## Mindfulness is not meant to 'work'

Having just spent time suggesting mindfulness will benefit you, it might seem odd to make a statement such as 'mindfulness is not meant to work.' This is quite a hard concept to grasp; we are trying to unhook from expectation or anticipation and to focus instead on experiencing the current moment as it is. To focus on the end result can only take us away from the present moment. The use of an analogy can help to make this a bit clearer. The common theme running through the following examples is that whilst the ultimate outcome might be desirable, the active pursuit of it will make it *less* likely to come about.

### 1 The argument:

Let's imagine that you have fallen out with your friend, and you end up not speaking. Another friend, who cares about both of you gives you some advice on how to patch things up; 'You know, I think it would be really helpful if you were to spend some time just listening to her side of the story, it might just help to take some of the heat out of the situation, and then perhaps both of you will calm down.' You reply, 'Do you think so? OK, that sounds like a good idea because I really want her to get over this issue. So how long do you think I should spend listening? Would 30 minutes do it? Or maybe an hour? Or do you think it will be longer? I need to know how long I have got to listen before she stops going on about this. Just tell me how many minutes you think it will take and I'll do it. It'll be worth it.'

Clearly anyone going into a discussion with this attitude is not really going to listen very well at all. They are far too focussed on getting the outcome they want. But even if this person *does* listen mindfully, there are no guarantees that the argument will subside. If you go into mindfulness looking for a specific outcome, it will prevent you from being fully present in the moment.

## 2 The first date:

It is perfectly reasonable that someone might want to eventually get married and have a family. But most people recognise the danger of starting a first date with this outcome uppermost in their mind. Once again, being focussed on a desired outcome would take you away from experiencing the true relationship. But even being fully present in each moment of that first date will not guarantee that this will be your life partner.

## 3 The soufflé:

What happens if you are cooking a soufflé or a cake and keep opening the oven door to check if it is cooked? The dish never rises. The action of checking alters the course of events. But even accomplished cooks who keep that oven door shut will sometimes experience a fallen soufflé.

It is hard for any of us to engage in activity without targets, expectations or guarantees, but it is exactly by attaching to those outcomes that your mind might catch you out. So when you have done a practice if you notice the thought 'that didn't work,' remember this point and remind yourself – it was never meant to 'work'. One of the hardest principles of mindfulness is to be able to pursue an activity without attaching to outcome. One of the greatest mindfulness teachers, Thich Naht Hanh (1991, pp. 26–27) suggests that we can wash the dishes *in order to wash the dishes*, rather than to get clean plates. How many times do we do something just to get to something else, rather than noticing that these are the moments of our life ticking away?

So here are some other things that mindfulness will not do for us; it will not stop our mind from wandering – only help us to notice that it has wandered and teach us how to guide it back. It is not relaxation – in fact, we go to great lengths to distinguish between mindfulness and relaxation, as we will see in the next chapter. It will not turn us into 'good' people. The central message is this; in mindfulness, we are not trying to *get* anywhere, but we are trying to *be* somewhere – in the here and now.

### Mindfulness in everyday life

When any new skill is learned, we have to transfer our ability to use the skill from the learning environment into the real world. In the way that we teach mindfulness skills, we are not trying to turn you into a meditator. We do not want you to be mindful only in the presence of a wise teacher in a special room with a 'quiet please' notice on the door, prompted to practise by the sound of a Tibetan singing bowl. The ultimate goal is that you will be able to be mindful at home, at work, out socialising or when you are on your own. In short, it is for all of us to be able to lead our lives more mindfully. So whether you are learning mindfulness with a one-to-one instructor, in a group or just from this book, prepare to practise in as many places as you possibly can, and to reflect on your practice afterwards either with your teacher or by yourself.

Here are some examples of mindfulness in daily living.

**Being mindful of the present moment:**

'I had to visit my sister 20 miles away. I am a nervous driver, and usually, I would be fretting about the traffic all week so that by the time I actually set off, it would feel like I'd already been travelling for hours! This week, every time I thought about the journey to come, I reminded myself: "I'm not driving right now, I'm not setting off until Friday." I saved myself a lot of worry.'

'I only had access to the kids at the weekend, and if I took them to the park, I'd remember when we used to go as a family. It would spoil the afternoon for me, and I'd end up snapping at them. Now I've learned to enjoy the look on their faces as they play on the equipment, and the sound of their laughter in this moment. It has really improved our time together.'

**Increasing mindful awareness:**

'I never used to notice when I was getting tense at work. Now I am more mindful of my posture, and my body tells me when I need to walk and stretch. My neck is much less painful.'

'If I was eating, I would always be doing something else at the same time; reading the paper, watching TV, chatting, planning what to do with my day. Now I focus on the food as it goes into my mouth and experience the taste and texture. I enjoy my food more.'

'I knocked over a carton of orange juice and my mind said immediately, "That was stupid." In the past, I would have got really upset, but I said to myself, "That's a judgement" and simply set about clearing it up mindfully – focussing on the feel of the cloth and the sight of the sponge soaking up the juice.'

**Using mindfulness to enhance effectiveness:**

'I could never talk to my husband about money without it turning into a row. Now I am mindful of choosing a time when we're not tired, and I describe the situation mindfully without making lots of judgements. As a result, we've been able to make proper decisions about how to solve our financial problems.'

'I would avoid telling my friends that my birthday was coming up, I used to think that if they really cared about me, they should remember. Then I was upset when they forgot, and so were they. I now realise that this just wasn't effective, I am much more mindful of doing what works – I send an email asking if people want to come out with me to celebrate my birthday.'

Can you think of examples of everyday situations in which it is hard for you to just be in the present moment without escaping into the past, judging yourself, making assumptions or predicting unpleasantness to come? Or can you think of times when you have kind of spaced out, daydreaming time away or just not noticing what's around you? These are all situations in which being mindful could improve things for you. In the next chapter, we will address how you start learning the skill.

### Key points to remember

- Mindfulness is a skill
- Use the internet, get tapes, articles and books
- Look up classes in your area
- Take your objections seriously, but don't let them stop you
- Identify times in your own life where mindfulness might help
- Note your favourite analogy – for example, your mind is like an untrained puppy
- Be aware of what mindfulness is *not* going to do
- Keep an open mind, be curious

# 3

# First steps in practising mindfulness

In previous chapters, we have described how being mindful can enhance the quality of your life and experiences. For any of us to get to the position where we can easily remember to be mindful on a daily basis, we really need to practise regularly in a disciplined way. This is why most people join a class or group, so that they can practise with other people and get some feedback on how they are doing. A mindfulness teacher should help to shape your practice so that over time you become more skilled at being mindful when you really need to be. If you prefer to learn how to be mindful on your own, you can begin by following the suggestions in this chapter. In that case, set aside a time each day when you are going to do one or more of the exercises we suggest so that you don't forget. We would also encourage you to practise being mindful at different points of the day, in different situations and in a variety of places so that you get used to being mindful as you go about your everyday life.

## What's the point of mindfulness exercises?

In a mindfulness practice, you usually have a focus for your attention, and you practise bringing your mind back to it over the period of the exercise. By taking some time for reflection afterwards, this short regular discipline can help you in the following ways:

1 You get to practise the action of deliberately focussing your attention (exercising the 'mental muscle')

2  You learn to accept the current experience ('being' in the moment)

3  You learn to identify the components of an experience (expanding awareness)

4  You start to notice obstacles to mindfulness (the antics of the 'untrained puppy')

5  You find ways to transfer the skill from wherever you practise to other situations (the 'roll-out' message)

In this chapter, we give some example practices and also some glimpses of what might happen if you visit a mindfulness teacher or mindfulness skills trainer.

### Keep it simple

Mindfulness exercises can be completely spontaneous. Here is an example of something you can do quite easily in almost any situation.

---

Right now, in this moment, run your finger lightly along the palm of your other hand, from your wrist to your fingertip. What did you notice? Was there a sensation? Is it still there? Did your mind wander off at all when you did that? Where did it go? Into the future? For example, 'I'll stop off and get some hand-cream as my skin is a bit dry.' Or into the past? 'This reminds me of stroking the cat this morning.' Or did it stay on the sensation? Were you judging yourself? 'I don't think I'm doing this right' or were you judging the exercise? 'How can this help anyone?'

---

In this instance, there was very little need to prepare, as the focus of your attention was – pardon the pun – readily to hand. But it contained the most essential ingredients of a practice – there was a chosen focus for your attention, and there was some guidance to help you expand your awareness.

Mindfulness is not about the highlights – it is about the spaces in between. When we seek to add complexity, we are rejecting the current experience, wanting it to be something other than it is. A truly advanced practitioner is able do the same simple thing over and over again – being as alive and awake the first time as the last. The real skill is to open ourselves fully to the moment whatever it contains.

However, being mindful in the current moment can be quite a hard skill if you have a lot of distractions. You are more likely to be able to achieve mindfulness if you practise regularly and in a formal way. This means setting aside some time on a regular basis and disciplining yourself. During these formal practices, you can add some ingredients to improve the effectiveness of your learning.

## Getting ready for the practice

You may be wondering where you are going to do your practice. If you are half way up a mountain in Tibet with a stunning view and no distractions for a hundred miles, this is an ideal location. If you are perched on a stool in your kitchen with the neighbours playing loud music and the dog scratching the door for his breakfast this is an ideal location. Get the message? Wherever YOU are is the ideal location. Whether you are sitting cross-legged on an antique Persian rug or on the 08:32 to Euston, it is still possible to choose a focus for your attention. The more demanding the distractions, the more difficult it is likely to be to practise, but also the more useful.

This is the reason that as mindfulness teachers we have never put notices on the door saying 'quiet please, mindfulness in progress'. Do what you can to make it easier for yourself to concentrate, but don't make easiness the most important thing. Most of us lead busy, chaotic lives. If this skill is going to be a game-changer for us, we have to make it fit the space we occupy. So let go of any judgements that your location is not quiet enough, or spacious enough, or peaceful enough, or tasteful enough. It is what it is. Your preparations don't have to be hugely elaborated, in fact the best exercises are very simple. So don't feel you need to rush out and buy a special cushion, or a bell, or a mat. But do arrange a space and time where your full intention is to practise.

**How to sit**

For this first exercise, we will assume that you have at least got a place to sit. Right from the outset, we want to be very clear about the difference between mindfulness and relaxation. It can be difficult to unhook from the notion that we should feel calm or relaxed at the end of the practice. For this reason, instead of trying to 'sit comfortably', we prefer the instruction favoured by Jon Kabat-Zinn to 'sit with dignity'.

Place both feet on the floor and keep your back upright if you can. We are doing the opposite of relaxation – reminding our body that we want it to be alert and alive. Try to keep your eyes open, just find a place to direct your gaze that isn't too distracting, perhaps a spot on the floor or on the table in front of you. Many people find it easier if they angle their eyes slightly downwards, as the posture of staring into the middle distance is often associated with daydreaming. Eventually, we will encourage you to be mindful in any position, but for regular practice, it helps to assume a posture associated with mindfulness.

These instructions might sound strange, you might be thinking that you want to lean back in your chair as that is more comfortable, or you want to close your eyes to help you concentrate. Remember the reason we are being mindful is so that we can bring this same quality of attention to our daily activities. Do you recall the girl in Chapter 2 who needed to take her coat back to the shop? She would certainly need to do that with her eyes open. Having said this, if you can't keep them open to begin with, don't beat yourself up about it, just work towards an eyes-open practice over time.

**Duration of a practice**

Mindfulness practices can be anything from 1 minute long to a number of hours. Our experience is that most people find it easier to begin with shorter sessions and gradually extend them. We have noticed in our own practice that we can become complacent at the ease of short exercises and assume that a longer exercise is just 'more of the same'. But this is not the case; there is a very different quality to longer practices; and we would encourage you to lengthen them out as you get more experienced.

Having said this, if you are someone who doesn't like to be alone with their thoughts, or if you feel your emotions very intensely, then 2 minutes might feel like a long time. When starting out, many people say that 2 minutes can seem like much longer. It can be amazing how many things your mind can do in such a short period of time.

When you start learning mindfulness, we would advise you to focus on something fairly obvious like sounds or objects. In the remainder of this chapter, we will outline some simple exercises of this type, and then in Chapter 5, we will move onto mindfulness of internal experiences.

As we introduce the mindfulness exercises in this chapter, we include scripts that we use when teaching a group or one-to-one. If you are practising on your own you can either read these to yourself before the exercise to give you an idea of what to do, or read them into a taping device and listen to them when you are ready to practise. After a while, you won't need this type of memory aid, as being mindful will become more natural.

### Key components of a mindfulness practice

1 You have a specific focus for your attention
2 Remember that it is normal for your mind to wander
3 If your mind wanders, notice where it has gone to and bring it back to the focus you set at the start
4 You may have to repeat the same action again and again
5 Despite your mind wandering, if you *return it*, you have been mindful

### Timing your practice

If you are a beginner to mindfulness then it is probably best to use a device such as a kitchen timer, a stop watch, a timer on your computer or on your phone. There are apps that can be downloaded to time the practice for you. For the next exercise, set your timer for 2 or 3 minutes.

**Mindfulness of sounds**

In this practice, we are going to be mindful of sounds. If you are able, then try and keep your eyes open, just find a place for them to rest. The task is simply to notice sounds that we hear. We are not attempting to label the sounds, although this might automatically happen. Our minds have been used to labelling sounds, so it is likely that as we hear 'tick tock', our mind may say, 'that's the clock.' Or if we hear 'dringg dringg', our mind may say, 'that's a phone.' If this happens, then there is no need to judge your mind for doing what it has always done; instead, just gently guide it back to the next sound. Whatever your mind starts to do, even if it goes into stories or memories associated with the sounds, the skill is just to bring it back to the next sound. Do this as many times as you need to until the end of the exercise.

The skill that you have just practised is that of 'observing', that is, noticing without having to put words on the experience. Try repeating this exercise whenever you remember it during the day. Repetition of the same exercise allows us to notice our own progress and to detect the factors that make our practice easier or harder. Listening mindfully is a good one to start with as it is a skill that can be practised in any location.

A mindfulness student recounted keeping a bedside vigil when her sister was seriously ill in hospital. She found that her mind constantly wandered into the future (fears that her sister would not recover) and into the past (the accident that had caused her sister to be admitted). During those long hours, she found she could not concentrate enough to read a book or magazine, and there were a number of other ill patients in the ward so talking or watching TV was discouraged. She turned her attention to being mindful of sound.

At first, she became alarmed, adding a label to each sound she heard, trying to work out whether it was good news or bad news (the sound of footsteps approaching: good or bad? A click from the monitor: good or bad?). But over time, she became more effective at just receiving the sensation of each hum, swish, click or whoosh that she heard, attaching to none and pushing away none. She found that her own sounds; her breathing, the creak of her chair as she moved position, became part of the experience of sound. Did mindfulness turn this experience into one that was pleasant? No. Did it make the time pass more quickly? No, but she stopped adding to her own distress by recalling the past or predicting the future. She found that she was able to tolerate the present moment more easily.

## Guided mindfulness of an object

This is a different type of exercise, one in which a teacher usually gives instructions throughout the practice. It is still possible to conduct the practice on your own, and we will give some pointers on how to do so at the end of the script.

For this example, we have chosen to be mindful of a leaf. (This is one of our favourite exercises as we work in the NHS, and leaves are cheap.) When we used to lead this exercise in a group, we would have a selection of leaves and pass them round the participants for each person to choose one. As they did so, we would say:

As each of you selects a leaf for this practice, I am going to hazard a guess that some of you are having the thought 'I want a good leaf.' The interesting thing is that for each of you, what would constitute a 'good leaf' is different. For some, a 'good leaf' would be one that is completely free from blemishes. For others, a 'good leaf' is one that is different from the others in form or colour. How interesting that even if you have never done this exercise before, your mind already has a protocol for it. Somewhere you have a mental file labelled, 'a list of qualities for a "good leaf" if you are asked to observe one during a mindfulness practice'. It is not just this current situation in which your mind has an agenda. It has millions of these protocols, producing them at the drop of a hat. Your mind won't wait for you to request the protocol, but it will just hand it to you as though these are the rules. In mindfulness, we learn to notice when this happens and then to exercise choice. We can choose to follow the protocol, or we can choose to ignore it.

### Mindfulness of a leaf

The following instructions will guide you through a series of observations. If your mind wanders off, then gently bring it back to the leaf and follow the next instruction.

First of all, hold the leaf in the palm of your hand. . . . Notice the weight of it. . . . How does it feel against the skin on your palm? . . . Are there places where it touches and places where it doesn't?

Pick it up between your fingers and thumb. . . . Notice the temperature of the leaf. . . . does it feel warm or cool? . . . Is it the same temperature all over? . . . Does the temperature change as you hold it between your fingers?

Notice the texture of the leaf. . . . Does it feel rough or smooth? . . . Do the edges of the leaf feel the same as the centre? . . . Is it hard or soft, firm or limp to the touch, damp or dry? . . . Does the stalk feel the same?

Allow your eye to follow the contour of the leaf. . . . Notice the shape and size. . . . View it from a variety of angles and see the shape change in your eye-line. . . . How thin is it, how wide at its widest point?

Notice the colour on the upper side of the leaf. . . .
See any variations in shade and texture. . . . Look at the
detailing; any veins, ridges, patterns? . . . Explore every
part of the leaf, the edges, the middle, the stalk.

Now taking the leaf in your fingers turn it over
and notice how the underside differs in colour and texture. . . . Notice how the light catches the leaf differently as you move it.

Is there a smell to the leaf? . . . Is it more evident
towards the stalk or in the body of the leaf, does it
change if you run your nail over the leaf?

Continue to use your senses to observe the leaf
until the end of the exercise.

If you are being mindful of a leaf by yourself, you can read
over the list of prompts to orient yourself on how the exercise
is done, and then set your timer for 3 minutes and explore
the leaf using your five senses. Alternatively, you can read
the steps onto a recording device leaving 15 seconds or so
between each step and play it back when you want to begin.
You might even do the practice with friends who are interested in practising, with one of you reading the instructions
while the others do the exercise.

Any object can be used for this type of mindfulness practice. You might choose to be mindful of something you see
every day around your home, or things that are found in
nature. Here are a few suggestions.

Stones, shells, crystals, acorns, pine-cones, conkers, twigs,
feathers, wheat stalks, flowers, fruit, vegetables, water,
raisins, biscuits, dried pasta (spaghetti is a particular
favourite for its projectile snapping qualities), cinnamon
sticks, sweets (those in a wrapper offer additional opportunities to be mindful), teabags, pieces of fabric, cotton wool,
sponge, pictures from magazines or birthday cards, keys,
buttons, stamps, coins, beads, toothbrushes, string, orna-
ments, marbles, CDs, coloured pencils.

## Mindfulness of the breath

Mindfulness of the breath is a universally recognised practice, and for most people, it is a gentle introduction to mindfulness. However, it can be harder if you have suffered from anxiety. You may find that when you turn your mind to your breath, you start feeling anxious. In that case this probably isn't the exercise that you should begin with, perhaps start with those exercises that focus on an object or listening to sounds. However, sooner or later mindfulness of the breath is a must for everyone, because the breath is something you have with you at all times. If you are someone who finds it difficult at first, then it is likely to be the one practice that has the most benefits for you, so please persevere.

Below is the script for a mindfulness exercise that we have used regularly with clients in the NHS, and it has two features that make it user-friendly even if people are naturally anxious. One is that it begins by directing the focus outside of the body and moves the attention slowly inwards towards the breath. The other is that it adds an instruction to label the 'in' and 'out' breaths. If you are anxious, this act of labelling can make the practice easier, but for all of us, the act of labelling helps us to focus.

---

### Mindfulness of the breath

Just take a moment to arrive here in this room. Allow the walls of the room to act as a barrier, keeping out whatever happened before you came into this room, keeping out whatever might happen after you leave.

Let's bring our attention to the way we are connected to this room, moving the spotlight of our mind to the very soles of our feet – can you sense the hardness of the floor beneath your shoes? And now pay all of your attention to the sensation of being seated on the chair. Notice how it feels to allow your weight to rest on the chair, feel the sensation on your legs and your bottom and your back as the chair holds you up.

And now bring your attention in further to notice that you are breathing. We're not attempting to alter the rate of our breathing in any way, but if it does alter, that's fine, just notice without judging. Bring the spotlight of your mind to the point in your body where you are most aware of your breath. This may be in your nostrils, or in the rise and fall of your chest, or in the expansion and contraction of your abdomen. Wherever that place is for you, see if you can tell the difference between the in-breath and the out-breath.

Notice that every in-breath is followed by an out-breath, and every out-breath is followed by an in-breath. Notice the point at which your breath changes from going in to coming out. If your mind wanders, then gently guide it back to the in-breath or the out-breath.

Now as my voice falls away continue to focus on the breath. It may help you if as you are breathing in to say quietly in your mind, 'IN', and as you are breathing out to say quietly in your mind, 'OUT'. Continue to do this until I signal the end of the exercise.

Learning to accept the breath however it comes is more beneficial than trying to avoid being aware of it, as the breath is with us at all times whether we like it or not.

**Mindful body scan**

Another universally recognised practice is the body scan, and there are numerous examples in books and CDs. The idea is to move the focus of your attention around your body. This has proved very effective for people who are suffering from physical pain. Recurrent pain in one part of the body, back or shoulder for example, will often draw our attention to the exclusion of everything else. This increased awareness can heighten the sensation of pain. One of our clients with post-operative pain told us that he used the body scan practice on a daily basis, describing the effect as 'diluting the sensations of pain'.

A further reason for practising the body scan is because our experience of the world comes through our body. Some people who have suffered from trauma have very little awareness of their physical self; they often describe themselves as feeling 'stuck in their head', cut off from their bodily sensations. The body scan can be a gentle re-introduction to genuine experiencing. This is a concept to which we will return in later chapters.

The body scan can be contracted or expanded but we would advise you to start with 15 minutes and build up gradually to longer practices. Some mindfulness teachers ask their clients to bring a mat and lie on the floor, but as you will have gathered by now, we think that sitting in a chair is fine too, as this is the posture you are more likely to adopt when you are using the skill outside of the mindfulness room.

---

### Mindful body scan

Doing a mindfulness body scan can be like being in a scanning machine, except that instead of radio waves, we are using our own attention to scan our body. While we are doing this practice, if you notice that your mind gets preoccupied by one part of your body, perhaps because there is pain or discomfort, then just try to treat that part as you do all the others, don't avoid it and don't linger there as the practice moves on. Just listen for the next instruction.

Let's start by bringing that attention to our scalp, right at the crown of our head.

Can you feel the skin across your forehead?

Perhaps you have the sensation of hair touching your ears or the back of your neck.

Can you feel any sensation in your eyes? And now in your cheeks?

Notice the feeling in your lower jaw – perhaps it is tightly closed, or a little open. Bring your attention slowly downwards, over your chin and onto your neck.

Notice the front of your neck, with the breath going up and down your throat, and the hollow of your collarbone, scan round and up the back of your neck, feeling your head resting at the top of your spine.

Now move your attention to scan the top of your shoulders, noticing if they are high, up under your ears or if they are hunched forward or sloping down towards your arms.

Move your attention to your arms, down to the elbows, then down your forearm to the wrist. Can you move your attention all the way round the bracelet of each wrist – how does it feel?

Now push your attention all the way through your hand to the very tips of your fingers and your thumbs. Can you feel any pulse in those thumbs?

Now notice your upper body, your ribcage and chest. Do you have any sensation there? In your mind, follow the sensation down your breast bone to the softness of the abdomen beneath. Notice the sensation down each of the little bones in your back, from your neck down to your waist. Can you scan around the girdle of your waist?

Notice the feeling of your hips and upper thighs. Feel your weight being supported by your bottom on the chair.

Follow the line of your thighs down to your knees, can you feel the chair beneath you? Is the temperature different on the back of your thighs to the front?

Bring your attention over the curve of your knees. Can you feel the hardness of your kneecap? Can you feel the skin over the top? Now notice the angle of your shins and calves as you bring your attention down towards your ankles.

Are you aware of any sensations in your heels, perhaps you can feel the cradle of your shoe around them? Notice the soles of your feet, and slowly drive your awareness to the very end of your toes, noticing the little toes on each foot and then your big toes. Notice if you have any feeling in the very tips of those big toes.

Notice that as you go through this practice, we are not asking you to change anything that you notice in your body. For example, we don't suggest that if you encounter tension in your back and shoulders you should relax your muscles or alter your position. This is the key difference between mindfulness and relaxation. In mindfulness, we accept what's there without trying to change it. We have produced a CD with a 5-minute breathing practice and 15-minute body scan – see the 'Other resources' section at the end of this book for details of how to order.

In each of the practices above – mindfulness of sounds, of an object, of your breath and of your body – we have shown you how to do the exercise in a formal way. But as you go through each day, you will have other chances to practise:

---

Listening to the variety of sounds as you prepare a meal – chopping, sloshing, sizzling and clinking.

Observing the sensations as you brush your teeth; holding your toothbrush, the feel of the handle, the sound of the bristles against your teeth, the smell and taste of the toothpaste.

Mindfulness of your breath as you wait in a queue to be served.

Mindfulness of your body as you rise from a chair, noting the pressure on your feet, the contracting of the muscles in your thighs, the forward motion of your torso, the changing position of your head as you make the transition from being seated to standing.

---

If you do any of these things with your full awareness and attention, they become mindfulness practices. Get into the habit of doing them as you go through each day.

You might like to keep a record or log of the practices that you do, as this is another way of encouraging yourself to practice. It is also helpful to see how you build up the time you devote to mindfulness on a daily basis – jot down any formal practices that you do and also when you have participated in your everyday activities in a mindful way.

In this chapter, we have described how to set up an exercise and given examples of some common practices. In the next chapter, we will look at some reflection that you can do after each exercise.

## Key tasks

- Keep it simple
- Clearly define the focus for your attention
- Only pay attention to 'one thing at a time'
- If the mind wanders off the task, just gently guide it back
- Start with short practices and build up over time
- Keep a mindfulness log

## Remember

- Mindfulness does not require a special location or specific equipment
- Mindfulness is not relaxation
- Be prepared to repeat practices, and also to add new ones
- Don't confine your mindfulness to one place and time
- Start to incorporate short practices into your everyday life

# 4

# Reflections after a practice

In Chapter 3, we described how to conduct some simple mindfulness exercises. Doing practical exercises like this will definitely help you to move the spotlight of your attention to a focus of your own choosing. However, you also need to develop the skill of being awake and aware of the actions of your mind. This is harder to do alone. If you have ever had sports coaching, you will know that your coach can see things in your game that you are blind to – the position of your head, the muscle tension in your shoulders. These things affect your performance. It is the same in mindfulness: your mind has quirks and habits that are unknown to you but that affect everything you do. Immediately after a practice is the best time to become acquainted with the intricate workings of your own mind.

## Reasons to do reflection

The function of reflection immediately after a practice is to:

- Appraise your current skill level
- Identify what you did that was truly mindful, and when you became unmindful
- Identify any obstacles that stopped you from being mindful
- Problem-solve any obstacles
- Shape your awareness of your mind's activities
- Help you to generalise the skill from more formal practices into your natural environment

There are three components of mindfulness that can be enhanced by reflection, and these might be referred to as the three A's: Attention, Awareness and Acceptance.

## Attentional control

This is the skill of focusing on one stimulus in the present moment, bringing the mind back repeatedly despite distractions from either the internal or external environment. Here are some examples of the sort of questions that would help strengthen this particular skill:

*Did my mind wander during the practice? Did I notice that it had drifted off? Did I bring it back to the focus? Did I have to do that many times? Did I get caught up in the thoughts and experiences that pulled me away from the focus? How long was it until I realised I was thinking about something else? What helped me to get back to the task?*

Being able to turn your focus of attention away from unwanted intrusions is the key to managing unpleasant memories, flashbacks, images, worry thoughts or other internal phenomenon. This skill is also useful if you have to tolerate noisy, risky or emotionally charged environments without rising to provocation. Imagine how useful it would be, for example, if when you were working in an open plan office you could tune your attention into the space immediately around your own desk.

Viktor was caring for his father who had Alzheimer's disease. His father would sometimes shout at him, hurtful remarks that he had never made before the onset of the illness. Viktor valued being able to turn his attention immediately away from those comments, to focus on his father's posture and balance, as his father had sometimes stumbled during fits of agitation. 'Before I learned to control my attention', he said, 'I would seethe about the unjustified nature of my father's words. Now I hardly notice, there are other factors I need to focus on to make sure he is safe.'

Viktor added, 'It wasn't easy to learn attentional control. I would set myself 5-minute practices each day using a CD of someone talking me through a breathing exercise. The first few times, I just turned the CD off at the end and went on with my day. Then it was suggested to me to reflect after each practice, and ask myself: "If it was hard to keep my mind on my breath, what made it so? What did my mind do instead of following the instructions on the CD?" These observations made all the difference.'

## Awareness of internal experiences

This second feature of mindfulness is learning to identify and label the different components of an experience; types of thoughts, emotions, sensations and urges. Just as an English teacher may help a student to label the parts of speech, you can actually learn how to label the activities of your mind. If you develop this skill, you will learn how transient those contents are, forming and disappearing from your mind like the bubbles in a pan of water on the hob, sometimes small and fleeting, sometimes big and splashy, either way, they make their way to the top and then are gone. In Chapter 5, we elaborate further on the different kinds of thought such as judgements, assumptions and interpretations.

Questions that can help shape your awareness after a practice are the following:

*What happened when I tried to attend to one focus? Where did my mind go off to? Were there any specific thoughts, images or sensations that cropped up? Does that happen a lot for me? How long did I linger on that mind content? Did anything happen in my mind that was not totally based in fact? Did I make any assumptions, judgements or interpretations? Did my mind impose any rules on me that I didn't invite? Did I become attached to things being the way I want it to be?*

In the following example, Nia has just done a 5-minute mindfulness practice where she was observing her breath. At the end of the practice, she paused to reflect.

> I notice that on this occasion, my mind did not wander as much as last time. I notice that my mind drifted two or three times at the start, mostly to things that I need to do later today. I was able to get my thoughts back to my breath, but when I had the thought, 'this is taking up time' I had the urge to stop the practice. I didn't though. I remember having the thought, 'this is a bit indulgent' and then another urge to stop. It's funny because I don't actually believe it is an indulgence, especially when it is for my health – I just don't know where that thought came from. I guess I often feel guilty when I do something for myself, but there's no law against that. I am going to try and be mindful of that thought if it comes up again, and remind myself it is not a fact, just a thought.

This is a good example of when the reflection led to an insight for Nia about how her mind works and enabled her to devise a strategy for when the same problem occurs again.

### Acceptance of the present moment

The third component of mindfulness is acceptance, sometimes referred to as turning up the impact of the current moment. In the following example, Dean has a lot of worries and his mindfulness teacher Ruth has suggested he practises mindfulness of the breath, but he has misgivings about doing so:

**Dean:** *It's no good trying to focus on my breath, I've got a heap of worries that I really need to be thinking about. I could lose the house the way things are going.*

**Ruth:** *That sounds like a serious problem. Does it seem as though hanging onto your worry thoughts is a way of solving it?*

**Dean:** *Or at least trying to solve it, yeah.*

**Ruth:** *(thoughtfully) OK, I see. So whenever you have thoughts about losing the house, do you immediately*

> *go into some kind of action that could perhaps save the house – like reorganising your finances or coming up with a new idea for a loan?*
>
> **Dean:** *No, because I already know what I have to do. I'm waiting to hear from the bank, and also about my job.*
>
> **Ruth:** *So at least some of the time the thoughts don't actually lead to any immediate progress on the house issue?*
>
> **Dean:** *Er, no, not really. . .*
>
> **Ruth:** *And tell me, on the occasions when they are not helping you with the house issue, are they still helpful in some other way? (Pause) Or do they sometimes get in the way of your daily routines?*
>
> **Dean:** *If you mean do they wind me up, yes they do. Then I get in a fight with my girlfriend. But it seems wrong to just let them go.*
>
> **Ruth:** *You know what? Our minds naturally go over things to try and solve problems, but they're not so good at turning this off when you have a plan and are waiting for more information to come through. I'm thinking that mindfulness might be a useful skill so you can turn your mind from those 'house' thoughts at certain times, and turn it back when you need to. We can keep practising the skill, and then you can try it out in those different situations and see how it goes. You've got so much on your plate right now, and I'm definitely not here to make your life worse, so if you develop the skill and then find it's not useful, you can just choose not to use it. But if it might help, then it sounds like you could really do with that bit of respite.*

Here Dean has to accept that there is nothing he can do immediately to solve his financial problems, but his mind has difficulty letting go. Anchoring on the breath is a great place for him to start, as it is impossible to take a future breath or a past one. Each breath can only be experienced in the here and now. Whatever else you struggle to accept, your breath will always happen in the current moment.

Here are Dean's reflections after the exercise:

I noticed that at first my mind still tried to focus on my debt. I just couldn't stop the thoughts coming. I wasn't paying attention to my breath at all. I noticed a thought – this is ridiculous, it's not going to save the house. Then as Ruth had reminded me, I just caught the sound of my own breath and that got me back to being able to focus on it. I started saying 'in' and 'out' in my mind.

I find it really hard that I am in this position with my finances, my business partner ran out on me, so it wasn't really my fault. I realise my mind goes back to that thought all the time. But for at least a couple of minutes, I was just in this room, breathing. It hasn't really changed my circumstances, but it has shown me that I don't have to keep thoughts about the house at the forefront of my mind all the time. In fact, doing that makes me feel worse.

Sometimes, it is an attachment that gets in the way of us accepting the current moment, as Francine describes here:

I was in a mindfulness group, and the leader gave out some postcards of seascapes and asked us to notice all the details we could see in the picture. I noticed another person had a picture of a beach I know well. My thoughts were full of things like 'I should have got that card, it's not fair, I don't even know where my own card is from, it would have been SO much better if I had got the other one.' In reflecting back, I realise I ended up not attending to either card, I was so stuck in my head. The teacher asked if when I get attached to an idea I experience intense sensations, and I realised that, yes, probably I do – and then get worked up if it doesn't turn out as I'd like. But actually, what did it matter? If I had accepted the card I'd got, I would have been doing the exercise with everyone else. I hadn't really understood before what the teacher meant by "unhooking" from what our minds do – but I can see now how apt that description was for my experience; I was really hooked into wanting that card!'

For Francine, the insight on 'unhooking' from attachments came not during the practice itself but through her observations of her practice afterwards. If this happens to you, it is important not to view it as a 'failure' to do the task, because the whole exercise should incorporate the reflection, and any learning that arises from it.

Earlier in this book, we used the analogy of 'the spotlight of our attention'. Imagine for a moment one of those huge theatre lights, the kind that might be used in a West End or Broadway show; with our three A's of **Attentional control, Awareness** and **Acceptance,** first we are learning to heave that spotlight around to shine on whatever focus we choose (Attention), next we're becoming alert to the mechanisms, obstacles and magnets that affect it's trajectory (Awareness), and finally we are learning to sit with whatever is illuminated in its beam, whether we like it or not (Acceptance). Reflecting on our practice as we go is a way of anchoring in each level of skill as we acquire it.

## Accepting help to become more mindful

To learn this skill alone is a big ask. It takes time and patience to see the intricate twists and turns of our own mind without recourse to someone who is more experienced, and who in turn learned from someone more practised than them. If you are working with a teacher, they can tailor their teaching to your requirements. In the following example, Joan has had a problem with social anxiety. In a group with other students, she has just done an exercise observing a pinecone. We have added some information about what the teacher is doing during the feedback so that you can see how she shapes Joan's awareness of factors pertinent to her anxiety.

**Tina:**   *So what did you notice during the practice?*
*(The teacher asks open-ended questions to elicit information*
*about Joan's experience)*

**Joan:**   *I noticed that my cone was black on one side, like it had been scorched or something. I wondered if it had been close to a bonfire.*

**Tina:**   *Did your mind hang out with those thoughts and images for very long, or did you get it back to experiencing the cone as it is, here in your hand?*

*(The teacher highlights how the bonfire image had diverted her from the reality of the cone in this current moment)*

**Joan:**   *I did get my mind back, it was helpful that you kept giving us more instructions, and that we were focussing on the feel of the cone and the colours we could see, but then when I looked at the black side of the cone, I just thought it was odd.*

**Tina:**   *So using your senses – listening to my voice and looking at the cone – was helpful in bringing your mind back. Having made an interpretation about it being odd, what happened next?*

*(The teacher summarises factors that promoted mindfulness and labels an 'interpretation'. She then draws Joan's attention to consequences.)*

**Joan:**   *I had the urge to look at everyone else's cone to see if theirs were black.*

**Tina:**   *That's interesting. Did you notice any emotion around when you had that urge?*

*(The teacher models gentle curiosity.)*

**Joan:**   *I guess I was feeling anxious, like there was something wrong with my cone.*

**Tina:**   *So as soon as you had the thought 'this is odd' you had anxiety and an urge to compare it to the others in the room? Was that a conscious decision – like, 'I know what I'll do, I'll just check out everyone else's cone?'*

*(The teacher summarises and then refocuses Joan's attention on the process, helping her to see that some of these mind-actions happen without her consent.)*

**Joan:**    *Not at all, I would much rather just look at this one, it just felt like a real compulsion to look.*

**Tina:**    *It's amazing how quickly we go from an emotion to an action without really noticing. Does that ever happen outside of here? That you feel anxious and then have urges to compare yourself with other people?*

*(The teacher links awareness gained in class to Joan's everyday life.)*

**Joan:**    *(Laughs) All the time!*

**Tina:**    *And is making comparisons usually effective for you?*

*(The teacher encourages Joan to be mindful of consequences.)*

**Joan:**    *Hardly ever, it usually makes me more anxious.*

**Tina:**    *So what could you do next time you notice the emotion of anxiety and the urge to make comparisons?*

*(The teacher restates the mindful descriptions of Joan's internal experience, giving her a language for these observations.)*

**Joan:**    *I'm not sure.*

**Tina:**    *You could just describe it mindfully, 'I notice I am having the emotion of anxiety' and 'I notice I am having the urge to make comparisons,' then refocus your attention back into the room. We could see what happens. (The teacher suggests alternative behaviour that can be done as homework and encourages Joan to be interested in the outcome.)*

Tina helped Joan to notice how quickly she moved into social comparisons when experiencing anxiety. Over time, Joan became more aware of this pattern, and when she became anxious, instead of immediately comparing herself with others, she just began to notice that she had the urge to do so.

If you are going to do this kind of reflection by yourself, then first you have to make a commitment to do some formal practices such as observing your breath, mindfulness of an object or the body scan. Then you need to make time after the practice to ask yourself some questions about what happened.

## Unhooking from attachments to one type of experience

It is perfectly normal to prefer pleasant experiences to unpleasant ones, but remember as you reflect on your practice that all your thoughts, urges or observations are as they should be – it is as it is.

After listening to music mindfully, Paul reflects in this way, 'I can't believe how much I got out of listening to this track. Usually I only play a CD while I am driving or using my computer. I never just sit and listen like this. I could hear harmonies that I never even noticed before. It was amazing, I really enjoyed it.' He then notices that he was so delighted with this experience that he had begun to evaluate it while the music was still playing, that in fact by saying those things to himself during the practice he missed some of the music. On another day, his experience was quite different, he noticed that while he was trying to listen mindfully, he had lots of worries about his diary commitments. When he reflected, he started to label those thoughts as worry thoughts, and this helped him to be more mindful in the moment rather than getting engrossed in each worry as it cropped up.

Although Paul was tempted to think that the first practice, where he really enjoyed the music, was the better of the two, his mentor helped him to realise that both experiences were equally valid. It did not matter whether his experience was pleasant or unpleasant, only that he was aware of what the experience was, and of what mind-events pulled his attention away from it. If Paul becomes attached to listening being pleasant, he may give up when it is not like that. Yet sometimes we gain more awareness and acceptance for ourselves when we let go of any agenda completely and just observe; here is pleasure, or here is discomfort. As the Buddhists are inclined to say: whether joy or pain, this too shall pass.

In another example, Corinne was practising eating mindfully for 5 minutes.

Afterwards, she noticed that the thought 'this is boring' had come along, and then she had some irritation in her body, at which point she had the urge to get up and find a magazine to read while she was eating. Normally she would have had no hesitation in going to get some reading material, but as this was a formal practice, she held off until the 5 minutes were up.

In her reflection, she began to wonder if the next time she had the thought 'this is boring' she could just observe both the thought and any urges and return her mind to her eating. A few weeks after this insight, Corinne had come to realise just how much she had the thought 'this is boring' and how whenever it came into her mind, it subtly manipulated her into changing her activity. It was as though it acted as a signal to give up on any given task. Now, however, she had some new reflections on that thought:

- 'It's boring' can be an assumption and when I turn my mind back to the task I find it's not really boring at all.
- It's possible to notice something is boring without judging it as bad, I can just agree with myself that it is indeed boring and carry on anyway.
- It can help me to be aware of this thought because it sometimes acts as a trigger for my mind to wander to other topics.
- It can seem like a very powerful thought that can stop me attempting to do a task, but it is still just a thought.
- I can treat it just like any other thought passing through my mind.

After repeated practice and in the light of her mindful reflections, Corinne was able to carry on with her activity even in the presence of the thought, 'this is boring.' As a result, she was able to concentrate more in college, particularly in the subjects that she found less stimulating.

## Reflecting as a stepping stone to everyday mindfulness

Remember that what we have been discussing in this chapter is doing set-practices for a few moments with perhaps a timer and a specific focus of our attention, and then reflecting on them afterwards to observe and accept as much as we can about the complex activity within mind and body. Later on in the book, we will see how to roll out these insights and our new awareness in order to enhance our everyday lives.

Over the years, some of our mindfulness students, most of whom have come to mindfulness as part of their therapy, have said, 'I can see the value of being mindful – I really want to be able to watch TV without having loads of worry thoughts crowding in on me, I want to be able to walk in the countryside and see the beauty of it instead of running through my to-do list, I want to be able to sit down with a few friends and not be so consumed by fears that they are judging me, but *really*? – To get that *must I* sit cross-legged on a cushion with a bell ringing? Or peer at a handful of acorns like I've never seen one before? Or keep breathing in some weird way, when I've been breathing all my life?'

The answer is *yes and no*. If you do deliberate, formal practices, then gradually, your mind is just more likely to respond to you when you want it to do your bidding. And at the same time you can also try being mindful while you watch TV, walk in the country or just stand in a queue at the supermarket, breathing. If you find the formal practices off-putting, remind yourself why you are doing them. It is not to get intimately acquainted with acorns! Your mind is like a constant companion, it wakes up when you do, and it accompanies you wherever you go.

During these practices and the reflection afterwards, you are learning more about this mysterious stalker and finding out that sometimes it hoodwinks you. It tells you that you can't do things that you subsequently do, it leaps to conclusions that are wrong, it gets attached to having its own way, and sometimes it reacts to things that either happened ages ago or that seem to loom ahead of you but never happen at all. Yet your mind can also be your best friend; warning you of risk, helping you appreciate the world around you, and coming up with brilliant, imaginative, creative ideas. Love it or hate it, you live with it. So you might as well find out more about your mysterious mind and become more adept at influencing its actions.

**Key tasks**

- Set time to conduct some formal practice
- After each practice ask yourself what you noticed; use some of the questions in this chapter
- Put labels on internal experiences; types of thoughts, sensations, emotions, urges
- Get as much insight as you can to what your mind does, without judging it
- Use your insights to help you be mindful in your everyday activities
- Seek out help from a group or individual teacher to hone your skills

# 5

# Being mindful of
# your thoughts

Mindfulness is about learning to take a step back and notice that thoughts come and go, without getting caught up in them. Do you ever find your thoughts race ahead seeing every possible negative outcome? Or you dwell on a mistake you have made? Or your thoughts keep going back over what you should have said and done? With mindfulness, we can just notice these are thoughts without getting onto the roller coaster of following wherever our mind leads. Wouldn't that be a great skill to have? When we take a step back from the thought we can more easily notice the consequences of it, for example that it can lead to an emotion, a sensation or an urge. So the thought: 'I have forgotten my keys' may be followed by a feeling of anxiety and the urge to check our pockets.

A thought is anything that passes through our mind. We might have thoughts like 'it is sunny outside' or 'I need a haircut' or 'my boss doesn't like me.' Thoughts can come as pictures too. If we are thirsty, we might see a cup of tea in our mind's eye, and this prompts us to get up and make a drink.

One problem in trying to step back and just notice your thoughts is that you may be thinking 'But that's not a thought, it's a *fact*.' Mindfulness is about unhooking from the evaluation of whether it is factual or not. We might have the thought 'the bus will be here in a minute'. Whether the bus arrives or not, at the moment this sentence crossed your mind, you experienced it in the form of a *thought*.

We've found it's easier to notice this with some thoughts than others. When someone has the thought, 'I'm going to get sacked for being late so often,' it might be easy for them to see that this is just a thought. But for some thoughts like 'I'm so ugly,' they might say it actually *feels* like a fact. Here is a common example:

> Janet was very anxious in social situations and would often have the thought 'I am worthless.' The thought seemed so true to her that she found it hard to use the mindfulness skills she was learning and notice it as a thought, allowing it to come and go. In their session, her coach pointed out that she could have the thought 'I'm worthless' or have the thought 'I'm a purple cat.' Both are thoughts. Having the thought makes her no more a purple cat than it makes her worthless. The humorous image helped Janet to take a step back, take a more curious stance and start to label 'I'm worthless' as a thought.

## Caught up in content

The main problem for all of us in detaching from our thoughts is the speed at which we get pulled into the subject matter without *consciously* deciding to do so. The following extract is taken from a session where the mindfulness teacher explains this to a small group of participants, starting with a personal example:

> I was at work and had the thought 'I have run out of milk.' In a flash, I was thinking 'If I leave work promptly and take a detour, I can pop into the corner shop and pick up some milk and still be back in time to meet the kids from school.' I had the thought and attached to the content without even realising it.

This fast processing can, of course, be very helpful. It can also cause problems when the content of the thought leads us to have painful emotions or to behave in ways we don't want to. Now, let's imagine the scenario again, with a different set of thoughts:

> I was at work and had the thought, 'I'm so stupid; I've run out of milk.' In a flash, I was thinking 'Why do I always do this? I never think ahead and I'm always forgetting things. Now I will be late and I won't be there when the children get home from school. How can I be such an idiot?' I started to think about all the other times I've messed up and felt really sad.

In the second scenario, we can see that instead of helping us solve our problem of having no milk, our rapid train of thought took us down a very different route. When we are being mindful, we do not assume that the first scenario is good, and the second is bad. Instead we learn the skill of 'stepping back'.

As you start to practise being mindful of your thoughts, just notice if you can identify any recurrent thoughts that take you down well-worn paths and away from the reality of the situation. Remember to try not to get down on yourself when you do this (this might be one of those paths!). When we are being mindful, we are interested and curious in what our mind does, and yours is just doing what all minds do.

## Choosing whether to act on our thoughts

In her mindfulness DVD, 'This One Moment', Marsha Linehan describes how early on in mindfulness training she would practise being mindful of her breath. During the practice, she would have the urge to quit and then simply stop. It was a long time before she realised she could have the urge to quit and just notice it *without acting on it*. Can you think of when this happens to you? A common example may be having the urge to eat something sweet, picking up a chocolate biscuit and putting it in your mouth in an instant. By being mindful of our thoughts, we can make a conscious choice either to follow our thoughts or not. So we decide whether we eat the biscuit, or leave it, despite the urge. Here are two more examples:

Beth had been bullied at school. As she grew up, she developed a habit of always doing things for others, so that she would fit in. Whenever someone asked her to do something, Beth would think they would only like her if she agreed. She would go to great lengths even though this often led her to feel resentful and to think she was being used. By learning mindfulness, Beth recognised that she was getting caught up in the content of her thought: 'They'll only like me if I do it for them.' She learned to become aware of her thoughts and notice the urge to do things for others without acting on it. Eventually she found the urge would pass and she could weigh up whether she really wanted to help out or not. She was surprised when some people liked her despite her sometimes saying 'no' to them.

**Personal anecdote:**

I had some feedback from a colleague at work the other day commenting negatively on the approach I had taken. I had the urge to jump in and defend myself, but I did not act on it. Rather, I told my colleague I would think about his comments and get back to him. On reflection there were some comments I agreed with and some I didn't. I was able to talk to my colleague in a much more balanced way for having been mindful and taking the time to decide whether to act on my thoughts or not.

## Unhooking from our thoughts

Once we have identified a thought, we need to learn the skill of unhooking from it if we are not to get caught up in it. We usually refer to this skill as 'letting go of thoughts without attaching to content'. Sometimes just labelling the thought will be enough:

Claire's husband was late home from work. She began to think about all the potential accidents that might have befallen him. Her anxiety was slowly mounting. Then she remembered her mindfulness teaching and was able to say, 'I am having worry thoughts.' Immediately, she felt as though she had taken her hand off a hotplate. The process of labelling the thoughts enabled her to let them go. As each thought returned, she told herself, 'That's another worry thought.'

Other thoughts can be much harder to release. We may make the mistake of trying to battle with the thoughts, leading to them bouncing back even more strongly. This is when the use of metaphors can be very effective. One of our favourites is a visual metaphor; here we describe how it is used in a mindfulness class:

'Thoughts that are really hard to unhook from are like "sticky" thoughts. The harder you push away the more they stick around. What happens when we "push" something?'

*(The class leader makes a pushing motion with her hand.)*

'What we get is the sensation of the thought "pushing back".'

'Let's see what happens if we try to loosen our grip on the thought instead.'

*(The class leader holds a tissue in her fingers, and then gently opens them, allowing the tissue to fall to the ground.)*

'But what if we have been doing some kind of craftwork and our hands have got some glue on them? We might open our hand but the tissue doesn't immediately fall. We have to resist the urge to wrestle with it, getting more and more covered in glue. Instead we need to keep repeating the same action until it eventually slides from our open hand.'

Metaphors that have a special meaning for you can be particularly powerful. For instance, a participant in a mindfulness group who loved to drive used to allow thoughts to come and go by imagining putting the thought in a car and watching it drive away. Transportation or motion metaphors are popular as they convey the concept of 'letting go' through the image of movement.

Here are some metaphors we have come across that you may want to try. They illustrate the 'transient' nature of thoughts:

*Being mindful is like standing on a railway platform watching the carriages go past.*

*Being mindful is like watching our thoughts go by like leaves on a stream, while we stand on the bank.*

*We can notice each of our thoughts like clouds floating in the sky.*

*Thoughts can be like birds flying overhead. We don't need to catch them; they will just fly on.*

*Watching our thoughts can be like scrolling through our email inbox; we can pass over some of the emails, noticing that they are there without having to open every one.*

The following metaphor is a particular favourite because it makes a number of points about the nature of thoughts:

*Sometimes our thoughts seem to come round and round again, like the food passing by on a sushi belt. It can be hard to let certain things go by. We may have a thought like, 'I'm stupid' and as it comes in front of us we are really tempted to engage with it. But beware! Every time we devour that thought, you can guarantee that someone in the kitchen is shouting, 'Hey, those 'I'm stupid' thoughts are going really well, let's get a few more of those on the belt!' When we are being mindful we watch the food pass by, simply noticing any urge to take it off.*

Using metaphors can help us to be mindful by creating distance between our thoughts and us. For example, if we are having trouble letting go of thoughts about an argument with a friend, we can bring to mind an image of putting the thoughts on a cloud and watching them float away. If we put all our attention on the picture we have created, then we are being mindful of the *image* of clouds. This is different to being mindful of actual clouds in the sky. To do that we would have to walk outside and pay attention to the clouds as they sail overhead. This might seem an obvious distinction, but if you are a person who has difficulties deciphering thoughts from facts, it is important to be aware that an *image* in your mind is simply that.

Jack hated school, and when he started work, he bristled whenever he was called into his boss's office about his work. 'I was right back in the headmaster's room,' he told his mindfulness teacher. 'No', his teacher replied, 'you never left the spot.'

For Jack, being able to distinguish between images and thoughts of school, and the reality of the situation he was in, helped him to move forward in his job.

**Practising being mindful of thoughts**

Before we begin some practical exercises, we want to highlight some key points:

- Thoughts can come as words or images
- There are no right or wrong thoughts
- We are not attempting to challenge or change our thoughts, just to notice them
- Opening our posture (e.g., shoulders back and lowered) can help us to open our mind

An exercise you could try right now is to simply turn your attention to the thoughts that are passing through your mind for the next 1 or 2 minutes after you have read these instructions. If you get caught up in the content of a thought, just notice and gently bring your mind back to the next thought. You can do this exercise without speaking, or you may find it helpful to say what you notice aloud as in the example that follows:

> I am noticing the thought, 'This is quite hard to do.' I am noticing the thought, 'I don't think I am doing this right.' I am noticing the thought, 'I should keep still.' I am noticing the image of my woolen gloves. I am noticing the thought, 'That was strange to think about my gloves.'

Another practice would be to notice the thoughts as before, but to give them a factual label. For example, a thought about the task, a worry thought, a 'keep still' thought and so on. In each case we are learning to take a step back from the content of our thoughts.

A common response we get after leading this practice is, 'My mind was so busy and then as soon as we started it went completely blank. There wasn't a single thought.' If this happens to you ask yourself: 'Did I have the thought "my mind has gone completely blank" at the time, or is it looking back on it now that I think that?' Often people will have had this very thought during the exercise without recognising that *it is a thought*. However, it is also possible that you did indeed have no thoughts, and then the aim is to explore with kindly interest the experience of having a few moments without thoughts. You may want to keep a note in your mindfulness log of your practice and experience so that you can notice what comes up for you over time.

### What am I if I am not my thoughts?

So if our thoughts are not facts, and we can notice them without attaching to them, we may start to wonder what this says about us. For example, one person asked, 'who is it that is stepping back from my thoughts?' The analogy of using the term 'my leg' can be helpful in understanding this. 'My leg' acknowledges that our leg is part of us, but not the whole. Just as we can observe our leg and acknowledge that we could exist without it, we can also observe our thoughts and see that we could exist without these particular thoughts.

## Thoughts leading to emotions

When you notice your thoughts, you may find they lead to an emotional reaction. For example, you may have noticed feeling happy and wanting to laugh or feeling sad and wanting to cry during a mindfulness practice. If this happens, try to take a gentle interest in your experience and the process that led to this. For example, it could be that you had a thought about a recent argument with a friend, felt sad and noticed tears pricking the back of your eyes. Mindfulness is about accepting experiences, letting them come and go without holding onto them or pushing them away, just like the sushi belt metaphor. When we do this, we can begin to notice links between thoughts, bodily sensations and emotions with interest instead of fearing or avoiding them.

This is one of the areas that can be challenging for all of us. People will often become attached to the idea that mindfulness should be a 'positive' or pleasant experience. They can find themselves making a judgement that if we experience a painful emotion, we have 'failed' or the exercise has been unsuccessful. In fact, the opposite is often closer to the truth. Is it ever the case that you find yourself going to great lengths to avoid certain thoughts or emotions? Whilst this may alleviate distress in the short term, does it ever cause you problems later? Learning to accept both the thought and emotion without fear can be hugely liberating.

Our advice is not to seek out practices to generate high emotions in the early stages of your mindfulness journey, but when an emotion naturally occurs as a result of the practice, to observe it and then gently bring yourself back to the focus of the practice. If this is difficult, it can be helpful to mindfully turn your attention to the physical sensations of being in the present moment such as noticing the floor under your feet and the feel of the chair you are sitting on, or mindfully observe five things you can see, taste, touch, smell and hear in the present moment.

## Categories of thoughts

People often find giving thoughts factual labels can help to take a step back and notice them as thoughts. By being mindful of your thoughts, you may find that there are particular categories of thoughts that you tend to have in certain situations. For instance, *worry thoughts* before going to a social event or presenting a report at a meeting. Keeping a log of your practices and reflections afterwards can help with identifying the types of thoughts and when they happen. Some very common types of thinking that are fairly easy to identify are 'catastrophising' (your mind going to the worst outcome or chain of events) and 'self-critical thoughts'. Two other categories that often come up are associations and interpretations, so it's worth looking at these in a bit more detail.

## Mindfulness of associations

Making an association between something in the present and something from a different situation is a natural thing to do. For instance, seeing a football and making an association with playing football in the park with friends. We rely on associations, for example, in a foreign country, we might associate a red cross with a pharmacy or medical help. But associations can sometimes cause problems. Here is an example.

Tom was waiting for a parking space at the supermarket. As the car pulled out another car approached from the opposite direction and took the space. Tom felt angry. He made an association with the last time this happened and he was late for a meeting, and his anger rose.

In this example, Tom now has to cope with the anger about the lost parking space today and also the anger about the lost parking space and his missed meeting from the past. If he had learned mindfulness skills, he could have noticed his mind going to associations with past events and brought it back to this one occasion of losing the parking space. Here is another example.

Jodie was an experienced mindfulness teacher leading a group mindfulness practice. She gave each person a piece of lavender and guided them to experience the lavender with all their five senses.

In the feedback, Fay said 'I started to smell the lavender, and it reminded me of being back in my grandmother's house which always smelled of lavender. It reminded me of all the happy times I had there.' Jodie asked if Fay noticed that this was an association. When Fay said she did, Jodie asked whether, when she had noticed this, she had brought her mind back to experiencing the lavender in the present. Fay replied, 'I noticed, but those were such happy times I decided to stay with it.'

Jodie acknowledged the desire to stay with the nice memories but asked if Fay would be willing to try noticing the association and bringing her mind back to the lavender in the present. Jodie gently reminded Fay that whilst on this occasion the association was pleasant, sometimes associations are painful. By practising returning her mind from a pleasant association there is more chance that Fay will have developed the skill well enough to use with a painful one.

By practising mindfulness, we are developing our skill in noticing that we have choices in how we respond. It is natural to want to stay with pleasant associations, but when we are being mindful we are awake to the present moment of our life and in following an association we have left this. A pleasant association will be a 'sticky' thought in the same way that a distressing association is 'sticky', so it provides an excellent practice opportunity. You may want to notice when you make associations and practise bringing your mind back to the present moment.

John had suffered from depression for many years. Through attending therapy, he had started to increase his activities and go to an art class that he really enjoyed. He went with his good friend Bob every week. When Bob moved to a different part of the country, John stopped going to the art class and became more depressed. When he thought of attending the class, he remembered how much he missed his friend and felt sad. He would think of all the times people had left him in the past and the pain of all these losses would feel overwhelming. He stayed away despite other class members phoning and encouraging him to come.

Using mindfulness, John recognised how the thought of art class triggered associations, not only with the loss of Bob, but also with many past losses and sadness that they evoked. He realised this pattern kept him trapped in a cycle of avoidance and sadness that felt overwhelming. With practice, he was able to notice where his mind had gone to, label it as an association and gently bring himself back to the present. With the help of his therapist, he learned to be aware of the sadness he felt due to missing his friend without the associations of all his past losses. He was then able to participate in the class once again, remembering to stay in the present moment of each session.

## Mindfulness of interpretations

An interpretation is the meaning we put onto an event. Different interpretations will elicit different emotional reactions.

Helen and her mindfulness teacher were discussing being mindful of interpretations. Jo, the teacher, described how she had sneezed when the group were being mindful of sound. She had then had the thought, 'I have disturbed everyone' and noticed the emotion of guilt. She then mindfully labelled the thought as an interpretation and noticed the guilt went down. When she was taking feedback from the group one of the other participants laughed and said that when she heard Jo sneeze she had the interpretation 'At last a different sound to listen to' and noticed the emotion of pleasure.

Helen told Jo about using her mindfulness skills whilst out shopping. She had noticed the thought 'They are doing this to wind me up' when a shop assistant was being very slow taking her money. She mindfully noticed the interpretation and was able to restate this factually to herself: 'I notice I am becoming tense in my muscles whilst I am waiting for my change.' She noticed the anxiety came down almost immediately.

## Mindfulness of judgements

An important category of thoughts that can cause difficulties for all of us is that of judgements. Being mindful means taking a non-judgemental stance. So what are judgements? They are a shorthand way of communicating. Saying 'That work you gave me was rubbish' is judgemental. It's a shorthand way of saying, 'That written report you gave me had lots of spelling mistakes, and the final section was missing.' Shorthand ways of saying things often don't tell us that much. For instance, if we said 'The film was really good,' it wouldn't tell you what the film was about or whether anyone else would enjoy it. A more mindful description would be to say: 'We really enjoyed the film because it had lots of car chases and fast action scenes that were very exciting.' With mindfulness the aim is to be aware when we make judgements and be able to restate them more mindfully or let them go.

When we are being mindful, we are unhooking from evaluative judgements such as good/bad, right/wrong, should/shouldn't.

Alec really disliked his co-worker Jim. One morning he saw Jim approaching his desk and said to himself – Why is he coming over here? Up to no good, snooping round my desk to see what I'm doing, trying to get one over on me. He shouldn't even be on this floor, I bet he's messed something up and wants me to fix it. By the time Jim got to his desk, it was as much as Alec could do to snarl, 'What is it, I'm really busy?'

'Oh, sorry', said Jim, 'it's just that you've left your car lights on.'

Judgements are not just what we say, but also the way that we say it. Our tone of voice, facial expressions and body language will all communicate either a judgemental or non-judgemental approach. It is important to be alert to the *internal tone of voice* of our thoughts, to help pick up whether they are judgemental or not. Changing our tone, expression and posture so we are non-judgemental in our bodies can really help us to let go of judgements and take a non-judgemental stance.

## Learning to distinguish between preferences, opinions and judgements

Giving an opinion is not being judgemental. Saying 'I really disliked that practice' in a neutral tone is an opinion, not a judgement. The person is just describing their experience – they did actually dislike the practice. If a participant in a mindfulness class says they liked the practise last week better than the one today, this is also their opinion or preference. It is fine to have an opinion and even to hold it very strongly, but if our tone of voice, body language or facial expression implies that it is therefore *bad or wrong* of the mindfulness teacher to lead such a practice then that would be judgemental.

## The consequences of judging

Judgements often push up our emotions.

Anya was in a railway carriage when some revellers got in after a party. She became disturbed by their noise and moved to a different carriage. 'I did the right thing, just walking away,' she said. 'But I was fuming for the rest of the journey.'

Her mindfulness teacher asked, 'Did you also walk away in your mind, or did you spend your time in the new carriage making judgements?' Anya laughed. 'Yes', she said, 'I was making a lot of judgements, so it is hardly surprising that my anger didn't go down. I needed to practise my mindfulness when I got to the new carriage, noticing the urge to judge, and bringing my mind back to the current moment.'

In mindfulness practice we are developing the ability to experience events, people, ourselves, objects and sensations in the moment without falling into the habit of judging the experience. If we judge something as good, we will want to hold onto it, and if we judge it as bad, we will want to push it away (like the sushi belt metaphor). Mindfulness is neither. Rather it is having the experience in the moment and then moving onto the next moment. Sometimes people will say they can understand why we might want them to unhook from judging something as bad or wrong, but ask why not make a positive judgement? The thing is that good/bad or right/wrong are two sides of the same coin. You can't have one without the other. If we judge some experiences as good then, by definition, some others must be bad.

The next trap for us to fall into is when we judge ourselves for making judgements. We need to just notice the judgement and let it go or re-state it factually. If you find you are making lots of judgements, and it is hard to let them go, counting them can help.

Mary was shocked in her appraisal to receive feedback that colleagues found her difficult and confrontational in her approach. She started to learn mindfulness and became aware that she made judgements about herself and others a lot of the time. She had always seen herself as having high standards but realised that this involved her constantly evaluating herself as not good enough in all she did. She would drive herself even harder with thoughts that she should be doing better and making more effort. She realised she would often have these thoughts about others as well and get irritated that they did not live up to her expectations. When she first recognised how many judgements she was making, she thought how wrong it was of her to do this. Her mindfulness teacher reflected that she was judging her judgements and suggested counting them could be helpful. Mary found this gave her the distance necessary to avoid getting caught up in judging. Over time, she was able to identify judgements sooner and let them go. Mary noticed a change at work with others being more friendly and willing towards her. At her next appraisal, her manager said that she seemed generally more relaxed and that colleagues had noted how she was much more approachable. Mary was really pleased.

A final point on judgements is about the use of the words 'should' and 'shouldn't'. Sometimes 'should' means *'in order to'*. This is referred to as a 'conditional should'. For example, I should get up at 8 *in order to* be at work by 9. Or I shouldn't go out tonight *in order to* ensure I revise for my exam tomorrow. Unfortunately, on many occasions we burden ourselves with unconditional 'shoulds'. We might say, 'I should be helpful to everyone, or I shouldn't bother people' without ever working through why we should or shouldn't do those things.

Tracey told me about a meeting she had with her son's teacher where she was able to use her mindfulness skills. Her son was having difficulties, and she was keen to sort these out and work collaboratively with the teachers. Unfortunately, in previous meetings she had a lot of judgements about the teachers and the school. These would increase her emotion and the meetings always ended with her becoming very angry, shouting at the staff and leaving before any plan had been agreed.

On this occasion, Tracey used her mindfulness skills in the situation, noticing judgements and letting them go or restating factually what the problems were. She was mindful of the associations with her own school days and how unhappy these had been. She noticed when she started making associations and brought herself back to the present situation. She recognised when her mind went to interpretations and checked out the meaning of what people were saying. She was mindful and present in the moment and, in this way, was able to stay for the meeting and contribute to the plan. This gave her a real sense of achievement, and she came away thinking she had handled the situation well.

A practice you may want to try is mindfully describing a situation that you found difficult recently. Notice if you are being judgemental in your tone of voice, facial expression, body language or in the content of what you are saying or thinking. If you notice judgements, then try to factually restate what happened or let them go and bring yourself back to relating the event. What did you notice when you did this? Did the emotion go up or down? What did you experience in your body?

Here are some other key tasks that are helpful to bear in mind or practise when developing the skill of being mindful of your thoughts.

**Key tasks**
- Recognise thoughts are separate from ourselves and practise 'stepping back' from them
- View thoughts as passing: they come and go
- Try keeping a log of your practices and be interested and curious in what your mind does
- Identify any recurrent thoughts that take you down well-worn paths
- Notice if you get caught up in the content. Remember you can choose whether or not you act on your thoughts
- Remember we are not trying to challenge or change our thoughts or make everything positive
- Identify common categories of thoughts for you, for example, associations and interpretations and practise bringing yourself back to what you are doing in the present
- Be able to recognise and let go of judgements

# 6

# Living mindfully

The ultimate aim of learning to use mindfulness skills is not to turn us into effective meditators, but to help us to live each day more mindfully. This means being able to experience each moment through our senses, and being alive to the impact of whatever it is we are doing. Most people can remember the impact of 'special moments' like holding a newborn baby, or their first day in a new job, or buying those boots they saved up for. It can seem as though the rest of our time is the in-between bit; just 'filler' between key events. Some people talk about 'me-time', implying it is a limited commodity to be squeezed into an over-filled schedule, and as though the rest of the time is 'not-me'. At one level, this concept makes sense – our minds have the ability to both create and inhabit a 'virtual reality world', almost like an out-of-body experience. Your body can be in one place, but your mind has already leaped ahead to the next appointment in your diary. The function of mindfulness is to help us to have more *in*-body experiences. Marsha Linehan describes 'participating' as one of the three major skills in mindfulness. In this chapter, we are going to look at the factors that inhibit our ability to participate fully in the moment and explore how to be more open to our moment-by-moment experience.

## Obstacles to mindful participation

Before we can engage in mindful participation, it is helpful to consider how being 'unmindful' might lessen the quality of our experience. The following examples might resonate with you:

Jeff is divorced from his wife, and their paths only cross when they meet up at family occasions, such as at their daughter's graduation. During these times, Jeff finds it impossible not to get fixated on memories of their split; he recalls in vivid detail the fights and the hurtful things she said to him. 'I realise that these memories spoil what should be a happy occasion. Instead of being able to focus on the happiness of the day, as soon as I see my ex-wife, I tense up, and then others around me can be affected too.'

Ayesha has her own business and three children at senior school; her life is a constant round of working, driving the children to various activities, helping with homework and looking after the house. She constantly multi-tasks: grabbing lunch at her desk, using the hands-free phone while driving, asking the children about their day as she prepares the evening meal. She feels as though she never gives anything her undivided attention as she juggles competing demands on her time. She recently had to visit the GP and found herself working on her notepad computer in the waiting room. She says, 'half the time, I am so busy I don't even know where I am.' Ayesha worries that she will never get to the end of her to-do list and start to reap the benefits of all her hard work, and that she is somehow missing out as her life rushes past her in a blur of obligations.

Becky told her mindfulness teacher how she had received a call from her friend one evening, who said 'A group of us from Uni were sitting in the coffee shop and you walked past; we could see you strolling along the pavement and we were banging on the window and calling out, but you were in a complete daze, one ear-piece in, listening to your music. By the time we made our way to the entrance, you'd gone, we even called your phone, but you didn't answer.' Becky was disappointed as her friend recounted the amusing stories from the reunion. She wondered how many other things she missed in the same way. 'The thing is', said Becky, 'I wasn't even really listening to the music. Sometimes I walk along in the same daze without my earphones.'

Do you recognise any of this? Has this ever happened to you? Can you think of an example of a time when you were unmindful when it would have been more effective if you could just have been in the experience of the moment?

Often when we point out what people are missing in this way, they tell us, 'But it is essential for me to multi-task; it is the only way I will get everything done.' In the case of Ayesha, if she did not do her computing in the GP waiting room, then when would she do it? And what is the point of 'participating' in being in the waiting room anyway, isn't it just dead time?

It is true that we can snatch moments here and there to cram things into our busy lives, and we do not want to change anything that is already working for you. We only want to enquire about *effectiveness*; what do we think was the quality of the computer work Ayesha did whilst waiting to see the doctor? What was the effect on her mood-state as she perched in the crowded seating area, writing? How do we think this might have affected her consultation with the GP, do we think she was more likely or less likely to recall all her symptoms or ask relevant questions?

It is sometimes incredibly difficult to hold your attention in the present moment. Try this exercise:

---

The next time you go from inside a room or building to outside, see if you can hold your attention on that moment of transition. Feel the door handle as you open the door, focus on the weight of it swinging open, notice the change in air pressure, see how the temperature cools as you move from inside to outside. Notice how the sounds alter as you step outside, notice the feel of the surfaces under your feet as you walk from one to the other – the sounds your feet make as they are in contact with that surface. Notice the shapes and colours you can see. What can you smell as you walk along? What do you notice?

We have sometimes asked clients in our mindfulness group to do this as they leave our clinic. Some clients report back that they had already 'lost hold of their mind' before they even heard the click of the door closing behind them. Their minds were filled with images of the drive home, or their shopping list, or perhaps some of the things we had discussed in group. Either way they were not 'fully in' the moment being lived.

## The time-travelling mind

Our mind has the capacity to reach forward in time to anticipate what is to come, or backwards to remember what's gone. Sadly, if we do not become more aware of this process, we end up missing out on a huge proportion of our current experiences.

Sometimes we refer to this as the 'time-travelling mind'. When were you last aware that your mind had 'gone' somewhere other than the present? Where was it that it went to? Sometimes we think about our mind visiting one of a group of 'islands':

---

*The island of past memories* – thinking about things that have happened. However, we do know that our memories are notoriously unreliable. Have you ever gone back to a place you used to live and been surprised by some component of it?

*The island of future plans and predictions* – beavering away on this island thoroughly believing that all our plans and predictions are like facts waiting to happen, rather than just ideas in our mind.

*The island of the fantasy past* – if only I had taken that job, if only I had remembered that important information. Our mind sometimes tricks us into believing that there is an alternative present that we would be living now had we just made the odd change. So remember the next time you engage in saying, 'if only' that you might as well add in 'and then if only I had picked the correct lottery numbers'. People often make a distinction between something that nearly happened and something very unlikely to have happened, as though the first is more 'real' than the second. But we cannot change the past; in this current moment of history, the fictitiously accepted job or the fictitious lottery win are equally unreal.

*The island of future catastrophe* – has your mind spent many an hour in this island drumming up a storm about something to come, only to discover it didn't actually happen? And even if it did – was all that catastrophising really helpful?

We need to notice that all these islands are in a different time-zone; when we hang out there, we leave the present moment.

This 'islands' metaphor prompted one of our mindfulness students to remark that whenever he had a holiday planned, he would spend all his time thinking about what he would do when he got there, and when he got there, he would spend all his time thinking about what he would do when he got back, so he was never actually *in* the experience of being on holiday.

Sometimes people object that if they are caught up in a memory or association of the past, and they unhook from it to bring their attention to the present moment, then this is somehow invalidating their trauma or their suffering. It is important for you to know that we are only suggesting you learn a skill, one that is designed to give the power back to you to decide where you put your attention. If you practise this skill, you can find that you are still able to access everything that happened to you – but at a time of your own choosing. The idea is that you are not way-laid by painful memories when you don't wish to have them. Then if you choose to remember, you can do that mindfully, too.

## Participating in the present moment – how close can you get?

The following exercise is another metaphor, this time hopefully it will encourage you to think about how much you really experience your everyday life.

This exercise is about experiencing football. What would be the difference between you reading a newspaper article about a match that is due to be played next week versus listening to a friend describe a football match he went to? Well for a start, the match in the newspaper isn't a real match, right? It's just an idea of one. The other match did at least take place, but your experience of it is via your friend and what he recalled of the match.

What about listening to your friend talk about that match versus listening to a match live on the radio? Well now at least the match is in the present, and you are involved as it is going on, but you are still having the match interpreted for you rather than witnessing it for yourself. So what if you watch the match live on TV? Well now you can see some of the match for yourself, although you are still seeing it through an intermediary – as you cannot choose to look anywhere other than where the cameraman chooses to show you. Do you think you would be more mindful of the football match if you were watching live on TV or in the stands at the football ground? Most of us would agree that if you were in the crowd, you would get a much fuller experience – the feel of the crowd surging, the chanting, and the smell of the pasty that your neighbour is eating. You can choose to pay attention to the players or anywhere else in the ground, but you would probably be more mindful of what was going on by being physically present. So what if instead of being in the crowd, you were playing in the game? How mindful do you think you would be of the other players, their position, each pass of the ball?

The function of this exercise is to get you to be more aware of when you are joining in with an activity, and when you are simply listening to the commentary of your mind. The trouble is that sometimes we mistake the commentary for the actual event.

> Yves was a landscape gardener, and one day, he was building a raised flower bed with a water feature for one of his customers. He had a clear idea in his mind of how he wanted it to look, but he could not get the materials together according to his plan. He ended up with a much less symmetrical pattern to the overall effect. He had to leave work before the homeowner came in from work. When his customer phoned that evening, he did not answer the call, fearing a critical comment. When he listened to the message the next day, the caller said, 'I loved the raised bed, the informal design really blends in.' Yves had mistaken the commentary of his own mind for the reality of the situation.

After one such discussion a member of our mindfulness group told us, 'I spend most of my life listening to a commentary by someone who never even went to the match, and doesn't like football!'

Sometimes when we are teaching this skill in a mindfulness group we have a number of exercises where we ask people to just throw themselves in, trying not to attend to the 'running commentary' of their mind. Here are one or two that you can do by yourself:

> Put some music on and just dance, if you notice worry thoughts about how you look or whether you are doing it right, just refocus on the feel of your body as you move. This exercise works best if dancing around to music in the house is just not the kind of thing you would usually do!
>
> Get one of those bubble-blowing kits that children play with, soapy liquid and a bubble wand. Blow bubbles

> and just watch them as they float and disappear; if you notice any self-critical thoughts, just return your attention to the bubbles.
>
> Set a timer for 5 minutes and count all the circles you can see in the room.

When doing these unusual activities, the reactions of your mind are likely to be more noticeable as you reflect afterwards – it is much harder to spot your mind's influence in an everyday situation. But when you get used to identifying 'mind-chatter', you can transfer this skill to more routine tasks.

What follows is an example of a typical exchange between a mindfulness teacher and her student after a practice of this type.

**Karen** *(mindfulness teacher): So what did you notice during that exercise (batting a balloon in the air)?*

**Sean** *(student): I got really competitive; there was no way I was going to let it drop.*

**Karen:** *And what happened when you had that thought?*

**Sean:** *I was up on my toes and my heart was racing every time it went near the floor.*

**Karen:** *So you didn't get distracted by anything outside of the exercise.*

**Sean:** *No, I was right in it till the end, I enjoyed it.*

**Karen:** *What happened to those worry thoughts you had when you arrived?*

**Sean:** *They went. But I was just distracting myself with this game. I mean, you can't do that all the time. I can't go around batting a balloon over my head all day.*

**Karen:** *That's true. So if you had spent this 5-minute period worrying, what do you think the outcome would have been? Do you think you'd have solved the problem you are worrying about?*

**Sean:** *No, my worries are not about stuff you can solve like that.*

**Karen:** *Hmmm, this is like that chess-board question – is it black squares on a white board or white squares on a*

> *black board? Did the exercise where you batted a real balloon distract you from your thoughts, or do you think your worry thoughts often take you away from the actual experience of the moment?*
>
> **Sean:** *I see what you mean, but I had something to physically do in this exercise, I'm often not too bad when I keep occupied . . .*
>
> **Karen:** *Maybe you can start to notice that you are always occupied doing something, even if it is just walking, or just eating, or just sitting. You could try bringing your mind to whatever your arms and legs are doing, instead of batting that 'worry balloon' around inside your head!*
>
> **Sean:** *It would help if I could, I'll have a go.*

Sometimes you might find that the injunction your mind gives you to NOT do something is so strong that you can't get yourself to do it.

> Leah couldn't get herself to dance, even in her kitchen alone. She kept having the thought, 'dancing's not my thing, I'm uncoordinated.' Then she thought, 'Actually, I don't like dancing, so I'm not going to do it. It's completely pointless.' As she left the kitchen she noticed that on the table was an application form for a job that she had tried two or three times to complete and then just abandoned. She realised that thoughts like 'I'm not good enough' had prevented her from filling in the form, and she remembered saying to herself, 'I'm not really bothered, I don't want the job that much, it's pointless filling it in.' She reflected, 'It's true that I don't like either dancing or filling in forms, but I can see that there's a pattern to my thoughts that are not helping me here.' Of all the things that she became aware of during mindfulness practices she reported that this was one of the most helpful.

### Real-life practices

At the other end of the spectrum from being mindful in unusual situations is the idea of being mindful in those that are the most mundane. Here is a description of someone mindfully filling the kettle to make a cup of tea:

*I am lifting the kettle off its stand and I hear a slight click as I do so. I can feel the coolness of the metal handle under my fingers, and the weight of the empty kettle as I lift it. I hear my footsteps on the tiles as I walk to the tap. I flick open the lid of the kettle and it makes another click. I see the shiny silver sink and draining board. I reach in front of me, feeling the coldness and the knobbly ends of the tap, with a degree of resistance as it turns. I hear a slight high-pitched squeak and then the gushing sound of the water, I see it coming out of the tap in a swirly column of bluish grey and feel the kettle getting heavier as the water rushes inside.*

We urge you to start being mindful of activities that you do regularly – can you make a bowl of cereal mindfully? Have a shower mindfully? Get dressed mindfully? How many things do you do without even thinking about them? When you make the complex movement to get yourself into a car, are you aware of the twisting of your body, the transfer of all your weight onto one leg, the number of muscles involved in your sideways motion as you position yourself squarely in the seat? It's a feat of human engineering, but we don't give it a second thought.

## Being open to all experiences, desirable or not

As you begin to live your life more mindfully it is inevitable that you will be more aware of *all* your experiences; some that are pleasant, but others that cause you pain. You might ask, 'Why would I want to be more aware of being in a situation that I don't like?' The following story is a very gentle introduction to the concept of openness.

Before I trained in mindfulness, I took my daughter, aged 5, on the bus. She was thrilled. She loved the jostling sensation, the disused tickets on the floor, the condensation on the windows, the smell of the diesel, she was fascinated by the other passengers, looking intently as each person pushed past us to get to a seat. In fact, she loved everything that I had come to hate about bus travel. What she loved, to sum it up, was the 'bus-ness' of the bus.

How sad that it should come to this. I would approach this experience with a list of what I considered desirable, and what was undesirable. This notion of judging the experience is not something that we are born with; children start with an interest in everything, they seek out sensations and novelty. But as we age we begin to become choosy, and if we are not careful, we gradually avoid a whole range of activities until only the comfortable ones are left. Our life becomes like a symphony without the low notes.

Here is another example:

I told a friend that I would love to visit the Taj Mahal. She had been there already and told me, 'You don't really want to go there; the terrible heat, the awful smells, the trinket sellers pestering you to buy stuff . . .'

But isn't that the **real** experience of going to the temple? Being there with whatever the sights, sounds and smells truly are? This is the difference between someone who has visited the real thing, and someone who has only seen it in a book or on film.

For many people, the experience of their actual life is not pleasant. At times, everyone has to deal with painful things.

Harold was severely depressed as his wife was dying of cancer. He was admitted to hospital briefly with depression brought on by the stress of it all. When leaving hospital, he was referred for mindfulness sessions. He learned to notice when his mind was wandering to the future, and to bring it back to this current moment, even though this was a moment of acute sadness. In doing so, he was able to stay with his wife through her last days. He later recounted that some of his most tender moments with her were during that time.

You might be thinking, why would anyone want to be awake and alive to moments of pain and sadness? Isn't it better to mentally distance yourself?

These are four reasons for staying with an experience, even if it is painful:

- We cannot maintain avoidance in the longer term. And when avoidance falters, as it inevitably must, we experience the impact of our pain more acutely.
- We cannot build our resilience without exposure to the situations and emotions that we dislike. When we fight our experience our pain gets bigger, when we experience it, we notice it passing.
- Pain is a natural part of life, and if we try to reject it we also miss out on meaningful activity, our world gets smaller as we try to stay in our comfort zone.
- We cannot solve our problems if we are mentally absent.

Sometimes we practise mindfulness of something unpleasant, deliberately choosing something that will produce discomfort:

Hold out your arms in front of you (if you don't have any physical health problems that would stop you doing this practice). Notice the urge to let them drop down, but keep them straight. Instead of reacting against the discomfort, notice what it is like and see if you can stay with it longer than you would ideally like.

Sit entirely still for 5 minutes. Notice any urges to move, even to swallow, and try to accept them willingly, but without acting on them straight away (it is ok to blink and to breathe!).

The next time you notice it is raining, stand for 2 minutes with the intention of just getting wet. Don't use an umbrella or cover your head or let your face pucker up or your shoulders rise. Just experience the feel of the rain.

When emptying the household waste-bins, do so willingly without trying to rush through to get it done quickly, or distracting yourself with other thoughts.

In each exercise, the active ingredient is willingness to accept the experience without rejecting or escaping from it. Here are some more examples to help you understand why this is necessary:

One summer there seemed to be a particularly large number of wasps around. Whenever a window was opened to let in some fresh air in the stifling heat, within minutes a wasp would fly in. Whenever Jess and her family took a picnic to the river bank, wasps would buzz around investigating all their sugary items. Jess hated wasps and was terrified of being stung, so she spent a lot of her time ducking and shrieking and generally being pretty miserable. One day she was at work and didn't notice a wasp that flew in behind her, stinging her on the shoulder. At first she was mortified, but as the pain of the sting subsided, she said to herself, 'Is that it? This tiny amount of discomfort that fades in minutes? I have spent hours of my summer trying to avoid just 3 minutes of pain.' After that, she made every effort to participate fully in the activity of the day, wasp or no wasp.

Greg was going through a court case with his previous employers. The interviews, statements and court appearances seemed to drag on forever, and when he attended court, all he could think of was 'I don't want to be here.' He found that his muscles were tense, and his answers were curt. He was consumed by the injustice of his position. Drawing on his mindfulness practice, he decided to fully participate in the court case, despite the fact that he'd rather be anywhere else. When he noticed himself tensing against the situation he allowed his muscles to relax and said to himself, 'I **am** here, there is nowhere else for me to be right now.' Instead of having to drag his mind to the proceedings, he willingly turned his attention to the person who was speaking, and listened mindfully. In his own answers he gave as full and frank account as he could. He released his attachment to things being a different way, and did each task to his full capacity. He noticed that people reacted to him differently, and he felt a sense of peace with himself that really surprised him.

Our final step in this journey of living more mindfully is developing the ability to discern the *richness* of our lives.

Henry was a war veteran. He was describing to his care-worker some of his wartime experiences in great detail, and she was engrossed in his account. He described some very traumatic incidents. As she turned to go, he thanked her for listening and told her, 'Those years were the worst years of my life, and also the best. We lived with the threat of death yet I have never felt more alive. We valued everything, even the ache in our muscles felt good somehow, like we were really working at something.'

Linda picked up her 5-year-old son from school, and they walked home together. She felt his slightly sticky hand in hers, hearing his fast excited voice recounting the day's activity. She felt a spot of rain on the back of her hand, and noticed the smell of the still-damp poster-paint on the picture he had handed her to carry. He stopped to stroke a cat sitting on a wall, and to point at a lorry going past. She reflected that in the past, these things might have irritated her, and she would have said, 'Come on, no dawdling, we need to get home.' But in this moment of insight, she realised that even though tomorrow would be another school-day, these exact circumstances would never happen again.

Living mindfully is the recognition that what is past has gone, and what is to come may never happen. This moment is fleeting, and by being mindful, we can allow ourselves to fully experience everything it has to offer.

**Key tasks**

- Notice when you are 'unmindful' in everyday life
- Notice when your mind wanders into the past or future
- Notice the capacity you have to be present in your experience or to avoid it
- Do practices that foster mindful participation
- Notice the commentary of your mind pulling you off track
- Be open to the moment even if it is not pleasant
- Accept your current experience

# 7

# Acting wisely

The idea of acting mindfully and making wise decisions runs throughout mindfulness practice. Sometimes it can be easy to act wisely, for example putting a tired child to bed when they have school the next day. Sometimes it can be hard, such as when our emotions are really high or our heart says one thing and our head says another. We might find an important work commitment clashes with our friend's wedding, and we are having trouble deciding which to attend. In this case, it can be helpful to use our mindfulness skills to help us work out what the wise decision for us would be.

The path to acting wisely follows the same path we have taken in this book. The first step is to be aware of our thoughts, emotions and sensations and recognise they come and go. They *are* transient. The next step is to be able to bring ourselves into the present moment and accept the actual situation as it is, rather than getting caught up in a *story* our mind is telling us about our experiences. From this perspective, we are not just reacting automatically to our experiences but are aware of the urge to respond and have choices about whether or not we act on this. As a way of learning the skill of acting wisely, it can be helpful to consider different states of mind and how they impact on us.

## States of mind

States of mind influence our behaviour and how we feel. Marsha Linehan describes three states of mind: emotion mind, reason mind and wise mind. The idea is that thoughts and behaviour can come from the heart (emotion mind) or from the head, that is the logical, rational, part of us (reason mind). Emotion and reason mind can be helpful or unhelpful depending on the situation. We will talk about wise mind later in the chapter.

Emotion mind is effective in situations where giving an emotional response enhances the experience such as hugging a friend who is crying or laughing aloud when watching a movie. By way of contrast, sobbing to our bank manager that we are overdrawn would probably be less useful.

Reason mind is beneficial where problem solving or a 'cool head' is required like filling out a job application or deciding on which route to take on a new journey. Reason mind is not as useful when you are listening to your favourite music or stroking your pet.

The idea is not that one state of mind is preferable to another. Rather, the aim is to be able to recognise which state of mind we are in and move flexibly between them so we can be responsive and effective in the situation. The following example demonstrates this.

In discussing states of mind with her mindfulness teacher, Jenny recognised that she was in emotion mind a lot of the time. 'When I'm in emotion mind, I just do things without thinking. I was in the shop the other day, and I felt so anxious I was sweating and thought my head would explode. I just wanted to get away so I ran out. I felt such a fool. I wish I could be in reason mind all the time, then I wouldn't have to cope with things like that.'

Jenny's mindfulness teacher acknowledged that reason mind would have been valuable in that situation and took the opportunity to help Jenny weigh up the relative merits of each state of mind in different situations. Jenny was able to identify examples of when emotion mind was helpful, such as having empathy for the elderly people she did voluntary work with. But emotion mind was less effective when Jenny was very anxious taking her driving test. She also recognised

that, whilst reason mind was appropriate when she was helping her daughter with her homework, it was less useful when
admiring the hand-made card her daughter gave her for her
birthday. Through this discussion, Jenny recognised that the
productive thing to do in the shop was to be able to move
fluidly into reason mind. The important skill was being able
to move between emotion and reason mind depending on
which was more effective in the situation. Rather than being
permanently in one state or the other.

You may find it helpful to talk about emotion mind and reason mind with your family or friends, as people will often
differ in terms of which mind they are in most of the time.
Their personal stories about when emotion or reason mind
was helpful or unhelpful to them can bring to life the discussion about each state of mind.

The goal is to be able to identify each state of mind and to
learn to recognise the cues that are likely to trigger emotion
or reason mind for you. For each state of mind, try to notice
the words you tend to say to yourself, the body postures you
adopt, your facial expressions and tone of voice (both internal and external) so it is easier to recognise them when they
pop up. Often changing your body posture or taking a step
to one side can help you to find the other perspective and
answer the question, 'What would the other mind say?'

### Finding wise mind

Marsha Linehan describes wise mind as taking into account
both emotion and reason mind perspectives. It is the middle path that brings together our hearts and our heads.
We experience wise mind in our bodies. It *feels wise.* Sometimes people will say they have got out of the habit of trust-
ing their instincts because they were told that what they
thought or felt was wrong or because they live life 'in their
heads' so much of the time that they have got out of the
custom of paying attention to sensations in their bodies. If
this describes you, the good news is that you can learn to

build your confidence in recognising your wise self again by following the suggestions further on in the chapter.

Occasionally, people will say they have never acted wisely in their lives' and don't have faith in their ability to know what is wise. In this case it's important to let go of self-critical judgements. When you do this, you will usually be able to identify times when you have done something wise or known what the wise action would be, even if you did not actually do it. Also you may be able to identify wise advice you have given to others. These are all examples of your own wise mind.

A common mistake to make is deciding whether an action is wise based on the consequence. An example would be the person who is in debt and finding it hard to cover the food bills, but spends £20 a week on lottery tickets. They may choose to spend less on lottery tickets so that they can buy food for the family that week. Even if the lottery numbers that they regularly choose subsequently come up, it does not make their decision to prioritise feeding the family any less wise.

If we were to ask you to answer this question, 'Have you ever behaved in a way that you knew at the time was *not* wise?' would you say yes? If so, this is your wise mind in action!

**Steps to wise mind**

Marsha Linehan likens wise mind to a wise friend. Here are six questions to ask yourself to help you be your own wise friend.

- Pause
- Which mind am I in?
- What would the other mind say?
- What *feels wise*?
- Be prepared to try again until it feels wise
- Give it time

A lot of people have told us they find these steps very helpful. You may want to put them on your phone or have them as a pop up on your computer as a prompt when you are in difficult situations. Sometimes people tell us they have them written on a card in their bag or pocket so they are always with them.

We have found these pointers particularly useful when using these steps.

- Remember to slow down and reflect as wise friends don't usually rush an answer
- Notice your body posture, tone of voice etc. to cue you into identifying which mind you are in, and change these to help you adopt a different perspective
- Notice where you experience the sense of being wise in your body and become familiar with that feeling
- Try to go over the steps more than once

Here is an example of how a therapist colleague of ours used 'Steps to Wise Mind':

On her return from leave Chloe, a fairly new therapist, found that her client (Ann) had responded very well to the locum therapists' suggestion to use mindful describing when talking to her boss about a problem. Chloe was filled with self-doubt. 'I've missed what was really needed. I'll never be a good therapist. My clients have missed out by having me as a therapist.'

Chloe had been practising mindfulness and used the steps to wise mind to help her think this through.

- Pause
- Which mind am I in? I'm in emotion mind, and it is saying: 'I'm anxious that I'm making mistakes and not doing the best for my clients. That I'll never be a good therapist no matter how hard I try.'
- What does the other mind say? Reason mind is saying: 'It was helpful for me to arrange for the locum to see Ann. It's useful to know that mindful describing works well for Ann as we can incorporate that into our therapy.'
- What feels wise: 'Being concerned about doing what's best for my client shows my commitment to them. Some anxiety is natural. It is unhelpful to criticise myself for it.

> There will always be things I can learn from other thera-
> pists and if I am warm towards myself and remind myself
> learning is a journey, I will be more able to embrace this
> rather than being frightened by it. It was a good call to
> arrange the session, and I can give myself credit for this.
> I can keep mindful describing as a potential strategy for
> clients in the future and use it with Ann now.

Marsha Linehan isn't the only person to have written
about different states of mind and how they can help us
to act wisely. The concept of 'modes of mind' is found in
Mindfulness-Based Cognitive Therapy (MBCT), and this
can also be useful.

## Modes of mind

In MBCT, different modes of mind are identified, that is
'doing mode' and 'being mode'. There are a lot of similarities
with Marsha Linehan's states of mind. For instance, the aim
is to develop awareness as to which mode of mind we are in
and to be able to move flexibly between them. The idea is
that both can be helpful or unhelpful depending on what
is happening. Awareness of the current situation gives us
options to think and behave differently. In modern Western
cultures, we spend a lot of time in doing mode, and this is
where we often get into unhelpful patterns of behaviour. The
skill needed is to access being mode more readily and move
between the two as required. Doing mode and being mode
are described in more detail below.

## Doing mode

Doing mode and being mode have different functions. Doing
mode notices discrepancies between how things are and how
we want, or don't want, them to be. Doing mode activates
problem solving to reduce or maintain this discrepancy. It is
focused on the end goal and is largely thinking-based rather

than experiencing the present through our five senses. When in this mode, our attention is often on what has happened (past) or what might happen (future). This state of mind is about changing something to make things different rather than acceptance of how things are right now (present).

Doing mode can be highly effective in helping us to solve problems but is less effective in helping us to experience the present as it is. If the problem we have is that we are going to see a film at the cinema, but we don't know when it starts or which bus is going to get us there on time, then doing mode is helpful in leading us to search the internet for the relevant websites and plan our evening. If the problem we have is that our partner of 30 years has died, and we feel intense sadness and grief, then doing mode will lead us to try to reduce the discrepancy between how it is and how we want it to be. This can result in us going over and over past events 'Why didn't I say . . .' or 'Why didn't I do . . .' etc. In this way, we avoid experiencing our emotion, instead getting caught in a cycle of rumination on past times or feared futures. In this situation, being mode is necessary to enable us to be in the experience and allow ourselves to feel the emotions that are a natural consequence of our loss.

## Being mode

In this mode, the attention is on experiencing the moment using all five senses, that is smell, touch, sight, hearing and taste. It is not just about being in the reality of pleasant events, but being present in neutral, distressing or unpleasant events too. It is about allowing into awareness our direct experience of all that life brings. In this way, being mode has a very different perspective to doing mode. Recognising the sensations in our body is an important part of this as it can provide a way to ground us in our experience and so help us to 'shift gears' into a different mode of mind. Being mode is not just experiencing our internal environment, but also our external world with information taken in through our senses.

**Which mode am I in?**

One way of recognising which mode you are in is to notice if your actions are directed towards a particular goal. Doing mode is about getting somewhere, for example achieving something or solving a problem. An example might be striving to get a promotion or pass an exam. In contrast, being mode means unhooking from the attachment to outcome. Being mode is acknowledging how things are, rather than trying to change them. It necessitates letting go of our minds' commentary on the present moment in favour of involving ourselves in the direct experience of it. An example might be playing ball with a child without worrying whether you are 'doing it right' or 'being a good parent'.

*Metaphors can be really helpful in explaining the difference between doing mode and being mode. One commonly used metaphor is that of a lake. Looking from the shore we can see the water is choppy from the wind. The undulating surface is like the activity of doing mode, reflecting the constant drive to make things different. In contrast, as we go below the surface to the deeper water, it becomes still and less affected by the wind. This can be seen as mirroring being mode. Both the surface and the deeper water are parts of the lake. It is not that one is good and the other bad, one right and the other wrong. Rather we are seeing the lake from different perspectives. In the same way, doing mode and being mode are different perspectives on our experience.*

Another metaphor that we particularly like is that of the road journey.

*When I go on holidays with my husband, we like to take a road trip. At the start of the holiday, we tend to be driving our car focused on our destination, our thoughts full of where we are going and how to get there. This is synonymous with doing mode. Contrast this with a point later in the trip where we are noticing the scenery when we pass, fully aware of the sights, sounds and smells around us. This example is more akin to being mode.*

The aim with recognising when we are in doing mode or being mode is similar to wise mind in that we want to be able to identify which mode we are in and be able to intentionally switch from one to another so that we can be making wise choices about how we respond to situations. Here is a personal example.

I love watching a well-known dancing programme on the TV. One evening I was sitting on the sofa at home when an advert came on giving dates for this show coming to my local theatre. Oh still my beating heart! I moved into doing mode. I was goal focused, my attention was on getting in touch with my friends and organising the trip to the theatre. There was a total lack of acceptance of my current ticketless state. My focus went to the future and how much I would enjoy the show and, on occasions, to the past. Yes, you will probably have guessed that when a similar show had been on, my lack of action had led to it being sold out before I had organised my tickets. This was not going to happen on this occasion. I was determined, problem solving and action oriented. Truly in doing mode!

Let's roll the clock forward to the night of the show. Imagine I am in doing mode. I arrive at the theatre scanning for discrepancies. Where are my friends? Should I have arranged to meet them here? Will we find each other in the crowds? What will we do if we miss each other when I have the tickets (no one was going to prise these from my grip until I handed them over to the attendant)? Oh, here is my group of friends, phew! Now we are at our seats, and I think we will see quite well. Or would we have been better with seats in the balcony? Would my friends have preferred the view from there?

How much do we think I am enjoying the experience?

Let's imagine a different scenario. It's the evening of the show, and I have found a parking space and arrived on time, thanks to doing mode. I realise that being mode will be effective in my enjoying this experience and start to focus my attention on information coming in from my senses. I notice the sense

of joy as I see my friends' faces appear and the smell of per-
fume as we hug. I'm looking at the gold on the balcony rail-
ings glistening in the lights and the sound of the orchestra as
it tunes its instruments. I'm aware of the chatter of voices and
the sense of anticipation as we take our seats. I can feel the
velvet on the cushion of the chair under my legs.

Which mode do we think is more effective in this environment?

But let's roll the clock back. If I had not been able to move
into doing mode when the advert came on and had stayed
in being mode, then I would have been acutely aware of the
sadness at not having tickets and the feeling of heaviness in
my heart.

So each mode is helpful or unhelpful to us depending on the
situation, and the skill we want to develop is to be able to
recognise each and be able to move flexibly between them
depending on what is effective in that moment.

### Effectiveness

Marsha Linehan describes the mindfulness skill of effectiveness as focusing on what works in any given situation. She
pointed out that we could get caught up in judgements about
what is right or just end up 'cutting off our nose to spite our
face'. Alternatively, we can be mindful of the situation as it
is, recognise the range of possibilities open to us and choose
the wise response. Without this skill, we can end up going
down well-worn patterns of thought or behaviours that
takes us right back to where we don't want to be. Have you
ever noticed those patterns in yourself? We have all done it!

Another way of explaining the skill is that some events
work out better if we are in doing mode and some if we are
in being mode. The art is to recognise each. If it's effective
to be in being mode, then be in being mode. If it's effective to be in doing mode, then be in doing mode. A useful
question to ask is, 'When is it helpful to act (doing mode),

and when is it helpful to let things be as they are (being mode)?'

In deciding whether we are taking the effective path, we have found it really helpful to look at our behaviour in the current situation and ask ourselves:

- Is whatever I am doing right now in this moment effective for me?
- Is what I am doing getting me closer or further away from where I want to be?

## Obstacles to being effective

In using this skill, we have found that sometimes obstacles get in the way of our being effective. These can be:

- practical problems such as the wrong equipment to carry out a task
- intense emotions, for example, being angry and not listening to our partner's explanation
- thoughts, for example, 'It's impossible' or 'I may as well give up.'

In talking to his mindfulness teacher about his thoughts, Tom noticed that he often had the thought 'I can't cope' when trying something new. When he had this thought, he would typically give up trying and then have thoughts about being useless and a waste of space. These knocked his confidence and made it harder for him to try new things. Tom had tried challenging these thoughts but could list several examples of how he hadn't coped when things were unfamiliar such as giving up an evening course he enrolled in, or going off sick within a week of starting a job. Using mindfulness, he was sometimes able to notice the thought and carry on with what he was doing, but other times he found it almost impossible to continue.

In the mindfulness group, Tom heard about the skill of being effective. When he noticed the thought 'I can't cope,' he would ask himself whether this was making it easier for him to do the task or harder. If it was making it more difficult then he would direct his attention to what would help in this moment. An example of this was one day when Tom was decorating his room. The paint spilled and splashed on the carpet. Immediately he had the thought 'I can't cope with this'. He had the urge to throw down his brush and give up. Being mindful, he recognised that this would not be effective for him as he would then have thoughts about being a failure and useless. The effective thing to do was to clear up the paint and continue with decorating his room. He knew he would need to mindfully let go of self-critical judgements to help him keep in the moment and not in the past when the paint had spilled.

## Lose awareness of the task

A common obstacle to being effective is being unmindful of the task.

A new colleague wanted to work longer hours so needed access to the building after the reception had shut. Thinking that this seemed like a reasonable request I asked the estates department to issue the necessary pass. The estates department refused. They had a quota of passes and were adamant no more passes would be given out. I felt this was unfair and continued to argue the point. The more I pressed my view, the more adamant they became. Until I asked myself the questions:

- Is what I am doing right now effective for me?
- Is this getting me closer or further away from where I want to be?

I realised that I was being unmindful and had lost awareness of the task. I had made my task proving to the estates manager that they were being unfair, but actually, this was getting me further from my aim of obtaining a workspace for my colleague. Once I recognised this, I could let go of my attachment to fair/unfair and focus on what worked. I was able to be open to new solutions rather than being stuck on one path. When I did this, I was able to see that there were other buildings that my colleague could work from after-hours where access was not such a problem.

You may want to keep a note in your mindfulness log of times when you recognise an attachment or judgement got in the way of you being effective or of when you were able to focus on what was effective in that moment and what made this easier to do.

You may say, 'Well leaving the party worked because then I didn't feel anxious anymore.' The task here is to be genuinely interested and curious as to whether this was helpful for you. It may well have been, if your goal was to stay at the party and leave when you felt anxious. If your objective was to stay at the party and talk to your friends however, then leaving the party was not useful in allowing you to do this. The skill of effectiveness would be to notice mindfully what was helping you to stay at the party even though you felt anxious.

**Mindfulness practice**

Here is an example of a mindfulness practice for effective-ness that we particularly like and that you may want to try. It can be fun to do it with others:

Each participant is given an egg and asked to balance it on its point. It is as well to note that the eggs are real and not hard boiled, so having some kitchen towel to hand is always a wise precaution. The task is to spend 5 minutes balancing the egg on a smooth, hard surface without breaking it or propping it up in any way. If the egg balances, the task is then to be mindful of the egg. If the egg balances and then falls, the task is then to re-balance it mindfully. If obstacles such as thoughts or emotions get in the way, then just notice the obstacle and bring yourself back to the task of mindfully balancing the egg.

There will usually be an array of responses to this practice if done within a group. Some people's minds will tell them 'it is impossible' or that you are 'trying to trick them' and the message will be so strong that they will not even attempt the task. Others will notice a competitive streak that makes them determined to persist and succeed. Still others will change the task to one they prefer, such as playing with the egg. Thus this mindfulness practice can help you to become aware of how the actions of your mind can either block or help you to be effective.

**Key tasks**

- Start to recognise when you are in different modes or states of mind
- Notice when each different mode or mind state is helpful and unhelpful
- Discuss this with friends if possible
- Practise using the steps to wise mind
- Develop flexibility in moving between modes or states of mind
- Stay mindful of the task you are trying to accomplish
- Develop the habit of being flexible in your responses and asking yourself: is this effective in achieving my current goal?

# 8

# From practice into everyday life

This chapter looks at how the topics we've covered in the book can work in action. Here are some examples of how people who have had problems have learned mindfulness in different settings and then benefitted from using it in their everyday lives. Points we have covered in the book are in (**brackets**).

## Sally

It was a foggy day when Sally set off to take her son Harry to school. Suddenly, Sally was aware of a flash of white to her right when a lorry pulled out of a side road and into the driver's side of her car. A passer-by pulled her son unhurt from the wreck, but Sally's legs were trapped, and it took hours for the fire service to cut her free. The smell of petrol stuck in her throat and made it hard to breathe, and she was terrified the car would explode.

Recovery back to health took a long while for Sally, with several operations and physiotherapy to help her walk unaided again. Sally would often cry with pain and frustration at how her life had changed and the fact she wasn't able to run and play football with Harry in the garden as she had before. Gradually, the physical scars healed and Sally was able to go back to her job as a clerk in the local planning office. She worried a lot more than she had before the accident, especially about Harry. She hated it when he was away from her and was reluctant to let him go to a friend's house to play or on a trip with school.

Sally's GP suggested learning mindfulness could help with the worry thoughts and explained that it is a way of taking control of your attention so you can notice when your mind has gone onto worries and bring it back to what you are doing.

Sally was not convinced that she would be able to do this, as her mind seemed to be caught in a constant stream of worries, but even a little relief sounded good and she was keen to try anything that would help. She could see her son starting to become anxious when she left him, and she did not want him to 'catch' her anxiety when he had always been such a confident little boy.

May, the mindfulness teacher, explained that Sally would need to do mindfulness practices regularly between their sessions (**importance of regular practice**). May asked Sally to try to do the exercises without constantly monitoring how she was getting on (**mindfulness is not meant to 'work'**). Sally loved to cook, and May explained that learning the skill of mindfulness was like learning to bake a cake. You need to practise and slowly it gets easier. If you are constantly opening the oven door to see if the cake is done, it will never cook properly (**use of metaphor**).

Sally and May started to do mindfulness practices together in the session. They began by observing a pen (**mindfulness of an object**) and using all their senses to be aware of it. May told Sally that her mind would probably wander when she did this, but when she became aware it had, to just notice where her mind had gone and gently bring it back to the pen (**normalising the actions of the mind**). Sally found her mind wandering constantly and felt frustrated that she couldn't hold her attention on the pen.

'It's a numbers game,' said May. 'You need to be willing to bring your mind back many times and when you do this you are being mindful.' Sally was relieved she was being mindful and was surprised by how much she noticed about the pen that she had never taken in before, even though she always kept it in her bag and used it several times a day.

'Not only can we notice more when we are mindfully observing, but we can also pay attention to what we are doing rather than doing one thing whilst our mind is somewhere else,' said May (**mindfulness is doing one thing at a time**).

'Imagine you are cooking tea for Harry while he is playing at his friend's house, and your mind keeps going to worries about whether he is OK and wishing he were back. If you were cooking the tea mindfully, you could notice your mind had gone to worry thoughts and gently bring it back to cooking the meal' (**generalising the skill of being mindful, into everyday life**).

Sally tried this the next time Harry was out. She paid attention to the sight, smell, sound, taste and texture of the food she was cooking and found the more she involved her different senses in what she was doing the more she could notice worry thoughts when they came up and bring her attention back to the meal.

Sally and May began to start their sessions with a mindfulness of the breath (**mindfulness of internal environment**). The first time they did this Sally noticed her breathing speeded up and seemed very irregular. She could feel her heart start to race and a sense of panic begin to overtake her. As she practised more, she was able to just notice her breathing whatever it was doing.

As Sally became more aware of her thoughts, she noticed how her mind would go down well-worn tracks and labelling that made it easier to notice and not act. May suggested she use the image of a luggage belt at the airport and notice the urge to take the baggage off, without acting on it. Just stand and watch as the bag goes past (**use of metaphor**).

Sally was doing the housework one day when her leg started to ache. 'If that lorry hadn't gone into me, it wouldn't be like this.'

'OK I recognise that luggage,' thought Sally. 'Just stand and watch the bag go past' (**use of metaphor**). Sally put her whole mind on the image of the bag as it went past her, watching it disappear into the distance. Then she put all her attention on the feel of the hoover in her hand and the sound as she vacuumed the carpet and mindfully carried on with the cleaning (**mindful participation**). Instead of getting upset and angry, as she would have done in the past, ruminating on the accident and how it had changed things, Sally felt proud of herself that she'd kept her mind on the task and finished the job.

Sally noticed a positive impact at work too and was really pleased when her boss commented how she seemed so much better. By noticing when her mind wandered, she was able to bring it back and complete whatever task she was doing. She felt like she was in control of her mind rather than having to follow wherever it wanted to go. She remembered May telling her that when we are being mindful, we do one thing at a time, and that this is more effective than trying to do several things at once. She found it helped to say to herself: 'In this moment, I am filing' or 'In this moment I am logging the application.'

Sally noticed she felt calmer and not so jittery all the time. By observing when her thoughts were racing ahead or going into the past she was able to bring herself into the present moment (**mindful of the current moment**). In doing this, she felt her body had come off 'red alert', and she wasn't watching for the next disaster to strike all the time.

May gave Sally a CD with a mindfulness body scan to listen to. May's voice guided Sally through the different parts of her body and asked her to focus her attention on each in turn. Sally found this very hard at first. She wanted to avoid focusing on her legs because they were stiff and painful. May encouraged her to treat every part of her body the same. Neither to ignore nor to focus on, rather to just notice each part as the spotlight of her attention came to it. Sally became aware of her whole body and that there were times when the stiffness and pain varied in intensity. She stopped trying to reject experiencing her legs and was able to be more accepting.

For Sally, part of accepting her legs as they were was noticing that sometimes she would feel sad (**mindful of emotion**) when the pain or stiffness stopped her from doing activities. May encouraged her to allow the sadness to come without rejecting or holding onto it. May explained, 'This is the mindfulness skill of participation, being "in" our lives even when the experience is painful or difficult because that is the reality of our life.' May told Sally: 'When we are being mindful, we allow ourselves to have the experience and also to let it go, have it and let it go.'

Sally would often think of the mindfulness story that May told her where we are at the door of our house and we welcome every visitor and let them in without judgement. 'We are going to let them come and let them go. Whatever they may be: laughter, joy, sadness or pain. We treat them all the same,' said May. 'We are not inviting them to sit around and stay for tea, but we are just letting them in and letting them out' **(metaphor/story telling)**.

## Skills used by Sally

Sally used a number of strategies described in this book to help her understand mindfulness and use it as a skill. First Sally needed to understand what mindfulness is and how learning it as a skill linked to her goal of being able to stop worrying constantly. This helped motivate her to keep going with it and try to use it as often as she could. It can be helpful to ask yourself: 'How would I like mindfulness to help me? What are my goals in learning it?' and write this down in your mindfulness diary. Sally needed to practise mindfulness regularly so that she could use it at really difficult times. As a keen cook, Sally often reminded herself of the metaphor of baking a cake to unhook from outcome (mindfulness is not meant to 'work') and be in the experience.

Sally practised being mindful of her pen and other objects as much as she could. When she found her attention wandering, she remembered that May's mind had done this too, and May had said mindfulness is not about struggling with your mind, but being willing to bring it back to what you want to focus on many times.

Sally looked for opportunities where she could use mindfulness in her everyday life to help her deal more effectively with her difficulties. She used being mindful of an object and the practice of noticing where your mind has gone and returning it to the task when she was cooking tea for Harry and worrying that he was not home. Sally labelled the thoughts and involved all her senses to increase the impact of her experience of cooking the meal. This helped Sally leave the worry thoughts and return her mind to what she was doing. Sally approached it as an experiment and started to be interested and curious about her experiences rather than always frightened of them.

As Sally became more practised in using mindfulness, she noticed patterns of thoughts when her mind would go 'down well-worn tracks'. The metaphor of the luggage belt helped her to not get caught up in the content of the thoughts and simply watch as they passed by. In this way, Sally was able to learn to bring her mind back from painful memories in the past or worries about the future and engage in the experience of the moment whether that was vacuuming at home or filing at work.

As is often the case, Sally and those around her started to notice a difference. Sally was willing to try May's suggestions, like the idea of noticing whether it was more effective to multi-task or do one thing at a time. She was really surprised by what she found.

Sally practised the body scan regularly and found the CD helpful. She found she could notice each part of her body equally rather than holding her attention on one part or skipping over parts of herself she didn't want (e.g. the stiffness in her legs). In doing this, she became more accepting of her experience as it is, rather than how she judged it should be. Learning to be willing to accept her painful and uncomfortable experiences allowed Sally to be mindful of her sadness without judging it as bad, trying to avoid or hold on to it. May encouraged Sally to notice the passing of time and used a mindfulness story to help her recognise that we can be willing to have our experiences and then to let them go.

## Mindfulness in a group

In the example we have just discussed, Sally worked with May her mindfulness teacher. Teaching mindfulness skills is often learned in a group setting, so it is helpful to consider this as well. A group may be held in any location, for example community centre, place of work, local college or school, Buddhist Centre, etc. In the example we give, the Community Mental Health Team ran the mindfulness group. What all these groups or classes have in common is an opportunity for people to come together to learn about mindfulness and practise some mindfulness exercises. Whilst some people may feel nervous at meeting new people, it can be really helpful to do it this way as participants can help each other and share experiences of learning a new skill. Hearing how other people got on can give us ideas of how we can use mindfulness, and it increases the range of practices group members can participate in.

Groups may run on a fixed-term basis where everyone starts and finishes together. Or they may welcome anyone turning up at a session and have no limit for how long you can attend. The example that follows is of a person who attended a mindfulness group that ran for an hour every week over 8 weeks. People could join at any point and stay for 8 weeks or 16 weeks if they wanted to repeat the programme.

### Dan

As Dan walked home from the mindfulness group, he remembered how hard it had been to get to his first session. He'd become so insular since he took medical retirement from the local college that even the thought of meeting new people had made him break into a sweat. But Pam, his wife, had been keen so she had walked with him the first time.

Dan hadn't always been like that. As a teacher, he'd been used to meeting new people every year. He'd been happy until changes at work meant he felt overwhelmed by the expectations on him. It was as though all his knowledge and experience suddenly counted for nothing. A reorganisation deleted his role and he became very depressed. His GP referred him to the local Community Mental Health Team (CMHT).

Dan couldn't remember much about the first group except that June (the group leader) had been very warm and friendly. She said it was a rolling group, so people could join every week, and some of the people had been there a little while. They smiled and said 'hello' and said they'd been nervous when they started too. June explained that mindfulness is about you being in the driver's seat, deciding where you want to put your attention (**definition of mindfulness**). She said our mind is like an untrained puppy running around, so we do mindfulness practices to notice where it has gone and train it to come when we call (**use of metaphor to aid understanding**). This caught Dan's interest. His mind was always going back to what had happened at work and how unfair this was. His confidence had been knocked, and he was frightened of new situations even though he longed to feel useful again (**link to goals**).

Dan liked the way June and other people in the group talked about using mindfulness in their own lives (**self-disclosure to aid learning**). It gave him ideas of how he could use it (**generalisation**) and made him feel like he wasn't so different from everyone else (**normalising**). At June's suggestion he started to talk to Pam about mindfulness and explain what they were doing in the group. They looked it up on the internet, and Pam seemed quite interested in the information. It felt good to talk to her like this.

Dan had been attending the group for a number of sessions now, and he enjoyed the rhythm of each week (**structure of group sessions**). They started with a mindfulness of the breath (**anchoring in the present**). Dan really liked this practice. It was the first one he had done and the one he used most often. When he was trying to get out, and his mind was racing with worries about what he would say or what other people would think of him, he would notice his mind had gone to this and bring it back to his breath. He would observe the experience of the air entering and leaving his body and the rise and fall of his chest. He liked that he could do this wherever he was. June would often say 'Sit with dignity' when they were doing the mindfulness practice to make sure she made the point that mindfulness is not about trying to relax, but about noticing our experience whatever that is (**distinction between mindfulness and relaxation**).

After the mindfulness of the breath, everyone would talk about the practice they had done during the week (**generalisation**). Dan had found it hard to talk at first as he worried other people would think his comments were stupid. When Dan was able to say this, he was surprised by June's response:

'That's a very mindful description. You noticed you had the thought, "They will think my comments are stupid", and you noticed that made it hard to speak. I wonder if you were to label it as a "mindreading thought" what effect that would have on how hard it is to speak?' (**modelling interest and curiosity, mindful of thoughts and highlighting consequences**).

Dan was pleased he had been mindful. When he tried labelling the thought, he found it easier to step back from it and just speak (**mindful of thoughts**). He did this when he was out with Pam's girlfriend and her husband and found it easier to speak then too (**generalising the skill**).

After discussing homework, the group would do different mindfulness practices. One week, June asked if anyone could remember what judgements were. Dan felt pleased that he could tell everyone they are the good/bad, right/wrong, should/shouldn't evaluations that we make. June asked them to draw a cow mindfully and notice any judgements they were making. They laughed as they looked at the pictures at the end of the practice.

'I judged myself constantly,' said Dan. 'The cow was all wrong, I should be able to draw properly. Why couldn't I do it when everyone else seemed able to?'

'Do you do that in other situations?' asked June (looking for opportunities to take learning from the session into everyday life).

'Yes constantly.' said Dan. 'I think it got worse when I felt like whatever I did at work was never good enough. I started judging everything I do and imagining everyone else is doing the same. I'm always telling myself it's wrong of me or I should do this or I shouldn't do that. It's so bad of me to do that all the time.'

'So you are judging your judgements,' said June. 'Hands up everyone who has ever done that' (**normalising**).

Dan was amazed to see every hand go up. 'I did that too when I started to notice all the judgements I was making,' said June (**self-disclosure to aid learning**). 'We all make judgements, but when we are being mindful, we just notice them and let go or restate them factually.'

Lots of people in the group said they had found this hard, but practice had made it easier. Dan was encouraged, especially when Terry told the group he had recognised he often judged himself and others. When he noticed this and began to drop the judgements, he was less irritable, which meant he got on better with people, including his wife (**highlighting consequences of non-judgemental stance**).

The last practice in the group each week was a mindful participation. The first time they had done this, Dan realised he hardly ever lost himself in an experience. He was constantly evaluating how he was doing, guessing what others were thinking of him, listening to the running commentary of his mind (**bringing into awareness**). Gradually he had started to be able to practise making a cup of tea mindfully, eating mindfully, walking mindfully, brushing his teeth mindfully (**mindful participation**). As he got more practised, he realised how much of his life he had been missing by living with memories and regrets from the past, predicting what would happen in the future or paying attention to his mind's constant chatter rather than being in the present experience. He noticed that one of the times when it was easy to lose himself in what he was doing (**mindful participation**) was when he was teaching, and he started to volunteer at a group for helping adult learners to read (**using the skill in everyday life**).

Being in the present wasn't always pleasant, like when he and Pam sat and cried at the impact his difficulties had had on their relationship (**mindful of emotion**). In using mindfulness, Dan was able to have the experience and let it go without it becoming overwhelming. He and Pam were building their relationship again, and he felt he knew himself better for all he had been through.

In the last group, Dan thanked everyone for all he had learned from them. Some group members agreed to meet for a mindful walk in a few weeks' time. Dan volunteered to lead a mindfulness practice and used pebbles that he had collected on the beach with Pam. He noticed the association when his mind went to the walk they had been on and gently brought it back to the pebble. As they left the room he turned to Tom, a nervous-looking teenager who had started that week and said:

'I found it hard at first but do keep coming. It's made a big difference to me.'

## Six months after group

Dan found that he didn't worry as much as he used to and when he did he was able to choose whether he spent time on this or not (**putting your attention on the object of your choosing**). If he struggled, he would think back to how other people in the group had encouraged him or described labelling 'worry thoughts' and bringing their attention back to what they were doing (**labelling thoughts**).

Dan still met up with the people from the group occasionally, and he practised mindfulness when he got up each day (**importance of regular practice**). He enjoyed varying the exercises sometimes doing mindful walking (**mindful participation**), sitting (**mindful participation**), or mindfulness of an object (**mindful observe or describe**). He still used the mindfulness bell app on his phone to prompt a few mindful moments.

Dan found mindfulness of the breath extremely useful in a variety of situations. It helped bring him back to the actual moment of what was happening, rather than his mind's version of it. Sometimes at night when he was trying to sleep and his mind was full of worry thoughts, he would bring his attention to his breathing and the rhythm of the in-breath and the out-breath as the air entered and left his body. When he was out with friends or meeting new people he used the skill of mindful awareness to notice thoughts like, 'they will think I'm stupid.' He found labelling the thoughts and being interested and enquiring when they cropped up, rather than getting down on himself, meant they had less impact. Over time, he was able to build the skill of being present in the current moment. Of course, there were still times when it was hard, but when he thought back to that first group session, he realised how far he had come.

By keeping up his mindfulness practice, Dan was able to continue to build on developing mindfulness as a skill and benefit from using it in a number of situations.

## Mindfulness in an individual therapy session

This vignette gives a detailed snapshot of an individual therapy session where a person has learned mindfulness and is applying this to a specific situation in their life. In this example, Sophie lives in a hostel but is moving out into her own flat. She has had problems with drinking in the past, but her goal is to stop drinking. We join the therapy session at the point at which Stan (the therapist) and Sophie (the client) are exploring an episode during the week when Sophie had been drinking.

### Sophie

**Stan:**    *So let's recap, you got back to the hostel after going with your social worker to view the new flat you've been offered. You were watering your plants and thinking how they would look when you plant them out in your own garden, and you felt happy. Then you noticed some other thoughts?*

**Sophie:** *Yes, I was thinking that I don't even know why I'm letting myself get excited; I will only fall out with the neighbours. I'll just mess it up, I always do. It will all go wrong.*

**Stan:**    *OK, and then your emotion changed to sadness, and that's when you had the first drink?*

**Sophie:**    *. . . and I feel really disappointed, as I haven't been drinking at all lately.*

**Stan:**    *Yes, you have done well, so I can understand your disappointment. So let's see if we can work out how we might have done this differently. Did you think of anything that might help?*

**Sophie:**    *Well, I thought of those mindfulness skills we've been learning, I thought I could have watered my plants mindfully, but I only thought of it afterwards.*

**Stan:**    *I think you're right; being mindful may have helped here. Why don't we practise now? Imagine yourself back watering your plants – you're going to have to talk me through what you notice as you pay attention to those plants. We've done this type of 'imagination' rehearsal before, so you know how to think yourself back to that moment in time. Now, as you talk me through your actions I'm going to say aloud those thoughts that were bothering you, and you are going to just notice them and gently bring your mind back to the plants. Remember to describe what you can see, or hear, or smell, or feel (**Stan guides Sophie in how to notice where her mind has gone and to bring it back to the focus of attention**).*

**Sophie:**    *Er . . . ok . . . this is going to be hard, but I'll give it a go (Client pretends to be watering some plants). OK, I'm paying attention to the stream of water coming out of the spout, and hitting the leaves. I can feel the watering can handle, and it's cold.*

**Stan:**    *(**interrupts, speaking out loud one of the problematic thoughts that the client had identified**) 'I'll just mess it up.'*

**Sophie:**    *I really will, that's what always happens . . .*

**Stan:**    *Ok, did you notice that you just got right back into that thought? Remember that we are going to use mindfulness instead, so the idea is to just notice the thought, and then quickly turn your mind back to*

> the plants. Would it help to say 'that's a thought'?
> **(Highlighting getting caught up in the content of the**
> **thought and suggesting labelling)**

**Sophie:** Yes, that might help, but it's still going to be hard.

**Stan:** You're right, these are really sticky thoughts **(use of**
**metaphor)**.

**Sophie:** Ok, I can see the water trickling down the leaves, and
smell the soil as it gets damp . . .

**Stan:** 'It will all go wrong' **(Stan plays the part of the**
**thought)**.

**Sophie:** . . . er . . . that's just a thought . . . I can see the pink
petals of the flower moving as I pour water around
the base . . .

**Stan:** Well done, you didn't get caught up in it that time.

**Sophie:** It helped to say 'that's a thought.'

**Stan:** One more try?

**Sophie:** OK, it's getting easier I . . . can hear the trickle of
water going into the pot . . .

**Stan:** 'I'll mess it up.'

**Sophie:** (more confidently) That's a thought. . . . I can feel the
watering can getting lighter as I pour . . . **(practising**
**labelling the thought and bringing her attention**
**back to the plant)**.

**Stan:** Great, you did really well. Do you think if you had
used mindfulness that evening it might have helped
you at all?

**Sophie:** Yes definitely. I'm just going to have to remember to
do it.

**Stan:** It's like a mental muscle **(use of metaphor)**. The more
you practise being mindful in your everyday life, the
more you are likely to do it when you really need to
**(highlighting the importance of practice to gener-**
**alise the skill)**.

In this instance, Stan chose to coach mindfulness skills
rather than go down the route of helping Sophie to challenge
her thought. This is because Sophie might well have been
able to give plenty of evidence of having fallen out with her

neighbours in the past. In fact, recalling her past failures may have set her off in further rumination about them. By using mindfulness, Sophie did not have to engage with the content of the thought at all.

## Mindfulness from a book: Ali

In this scenario Ali is teaching herself mindfulness using suggestions from this book.

Ali always seemed to be rushing from one thing to the next. She felt stressed at work and stressed at home. Splitting up with her boyfriend had really knocked her confidence. One day, she was in the newsagent when she saw a book on mindfulness and picked it up to have a look. She'd read a bit about mindfulness and seen some things on the TV and thought it might be interesting to find out more.

The book said mindfulness is being in control of your mind instead of your mind being in control of you (**definition of mindfulness**). Ali was curious and decided to give it a go. She wanted a new boyfriend and thought this would go better if she wasn't so stressed all the time (**link to goals**). It made sense to her that to benefit from using mindfulness she would need to practise (**importance of regular practice**). She could vividly remember the first time she tried it. With the book propped in front of her she had read through what she needed to do, set the timer on her phone for 2 minutes, and then, sitting upright in her chair looking down at the carpet, she listened to the sounds in the room (**mindful observation of external environment**). She'd been aware of so many thoughts, wondering if she was doing it right, worrying that she wasn't and wondering when it would end. But she'd also managed to focus on the sound of the fridge whirring in the background and the cars passing by outside. Afterwards, she'd written the practice in her mindfulness log and made a note that she had read in the book: 'When you notice your mind had wandered onto thoughts and bring it back to sounds, you are being mindful.' So she thought she'd done OK.

Ali really enjoyed trying the different practices from the book. She decided to mindfully brush her teeth each morning (**mindful participation**) and had a go at doing an exercise from the book most evenings whether that was mindfully reading an email (**mindful participation**), mindfully drinking her tea (**mindful participation**) or mindfully looking at a leaf (**mindfulness of an object**). She taped herself reading the scripts from the book and sometimes used these to guide her (**varying practices**).

Ali wrote her mindfulness log each evening (**reflections on mindfulness practice**) and noticed sometimes it was easier to be mindful than others and certain patterns coming up time and again. For instance, when she focused on her breathing in a mindfulness practice, she started thinking how fast it was and that it couldn't be natural. She felt her heartbeat increase and thought: 'this can't be good for me.' She had the urge to stop and did. She realised she often felt anxious when she became aware of changes in her body and usually coped by distracting herself when this happened. She read the book to see if it gave advice about this and was interested that it said mindfulness is about accepting our experiences whatever they are and how we can have the urge to do something and just notice the urge without acting on it. It took her a while to go back to being mindful of her breath, but when she did, she tried noticing and labelling the thoughts that came up and not acting on the urge to quit (**labelling thoughts and urges without getting caught up in content**). She was surprised that the more she did this, the easier it got. She started being mindful of her breath at other times, like when things she had to get done were piling in on her. By focusing on her breath, it brought her into the moment of her life rather than being caught up in the story her mind was telling her, and then she would mindfully focus on whatever she was doing (**generalising the skill of being mindful into everyday life**). Ali liked the football metaphor from the book and would remind herself: 'This is my arms and legs life. I'm on the pitch rather than listening to a commentary about a game that may never happen!' (**use of metaphor, participating in your actual life**).

Another pattern Ali noticed was making judgements. She was quite horrified when she realised how much of her time she spent judging (**judging her judgements**). She realised her mind would often replay what she should have said and done, or think that others should know how she was feeling or shouldn't behave in a particular way (**noticing judgements**). Ali found counting the judgements or saying factually what she meant often took the heat out of a situation or helped her think about it differently (**taking a non-judgemental stance**). This was really useful when she met her new boyfriend and her mind would go into the future, judging that things would go wrong just as they had before. She was able to label the judgements and notice her mind had left for 'future island' (**use of metaphor**) and smiled to herself remembering the piece in the book which said: 'if we are going to make up the future, we may as well put in a lottery win.'

Ali found mindfulness helpful at work too. She noticed she was more effective when she did one thing at a time and felt a lot less stressed. Over time, she realised she was involving herself in whatever she was doing rather than just following when her mind raced onto everything she had to do (**participating more mindfully in her life**). When her friend commented on how Ali seemed happier in herself, Ali lent them her mindfulness book saying: 'give it a go, I wouldn't have believed the difference it made to me.'

## Conclusion

Sally, Dan, Sophie and Ali have shown how the topics in this book come together to enable people to learn mindfulness skills and use them in their everyday lives. Whether mindfulness is learned from reading a book, in a class or individually with a mindfulness teacher, our experience is that using these skills have often had a profound impact on people, enhancing their ability to deal more effectively with the problems they encounter.

**Key tasks**

- Explore information about mindfulness from, for example, books, TV, internet etc.
- Remind yourself how using mindfulness as a skill links to your goals
- Vary your practices
- Keep a record of your practices and learning in your mindfulness log
- Look for opportunities to generalise mindfulness into your everyday life

# Concluding comments

Finally, we want to say that we have found mindfulness skills have enriched our lives, helped us cope when times are difficult and enhanced the experience when things are going well. We hope that this is your experience too and want to wish you every success in using mindfulness skills and participating fully in the actual moment of your life, whatever that may be.

# Other resources

## Books about mindfulness

Dunkley, C. and Stanton, M. (2014) *Teaching Clients to Use Mindfulness Skills: A Practical Guide*. London & New York: Routledge.

Hanh, T. N. (2008) *The Miracle of Mindfulness: The Classic Guide to Meditation by the World's Most Revered Master*. London: Rider, Ebury Publishing, Random House Company.

Hanh, T. N. (1991) *Peace Is Every Step: The Path of Mindfulness in Everyday Life*. London: Rider.

Hawn, G. with Holden, W. (2012) *10 Mindful Minutes*. London: Piatkus.

Kabat-Zinn, J. (1994) *Wherever You Go, There You Are: Mindfulness Meditation for Everyday Life*. London: Piatkus Books.

Kabat-Zinn, J. (1990) *Full Catastrophe Living: How to Cope With Stress, Pain and Illness Using Mindfulness Meditation*. London: Piatkus Books.

Kozak, A. (2009) *Wild Chickens and Petty Tyrants: 108 Metaphors for Mindfulness*. Boston: Wisdom.

Linehan, M. (1993) *Cognitive-behavioral Treatment of Borderline Personality Disorder*. New York: Guilford Press.

## Internet resources

These links have been checked at the time of going to print.

Kabat-Zinn, J. (2007) leads a session on Mindfulness at Google 72 min – Uploaded by Google
www.youtube.com/watch?v=3nwwKbM_vJc

Be mindful website offers information on mindfulness, classes and teachers
www.bemindful.co.uk

Headspace website offers online meditation courses and apps
www.headspace.co.uk

Sillito, D. (2012) Mind over matter: Can meditation bring happiness? BBC News 4.1.12
www.bbc.co.uk/news/health-16389183

Mitchell, T. (2016) Edited by Longyear, S. Mindfulness: The practice of "being here now".
www.working-well.org/articles/pdf/Mindfulness.pdf

DVD (1995) *This One Moment: Skills for Everyday Mindfulness.* See Marsha Linehan teaching mindfulness skills. Produced by Behavioral Tech LLC order from
http://behavioraltech.org

Audio CD by the authors with a 5 minute breathing exercise and 15 minute body scan from either
www.stantonltd.co.uk/product.php?xProd=182&xSec=2 or http://bit.ly/grayrockCD

Mindfulness Bells handcrafted in Nepal from either
http://bit.ly/grayrockbell or
www.stantonltd.co.uk/product.php?xProd=29&xSec=2

# Index